A Reappraisal of Marxian Economics

A Reappraisal of
Marxian Economics

By Murray Wolfson

COLUMBIA UNIVERSITY PRESS

NEW YORK AND LONDON · 1966

Murray Wolfson is Assistant Professor of Economics at Oregon State University.

To Betty, Paul, Susan, and Deborah
and to the common sense of ordinary people

Preface

The critic's task is to put Marx to the test of the scientific method. Where he has made a meaningful prediction we can examine the evidence and decide if it is falsified by the facts. Where his concepts are not falsifiable in principle they can be declared metaphysical lumber and discarded.

But having made the resolve we find ourselves in no small difficulty. Statistical testing of the Marxian predictions have been notoriously unsuccessful in arriving at significant conclusions. That the concepts themselves were not designed for econometric purposes will become apparent in discussing Marx's theory of value. Furthermore, their validity can only be established on the basis of international aggregates which presents formidable statistical difficulties. More important than this, Marx made very few firm predictions, but spoke of tendencies and countertendencies. While it usually is evident what tendency he expected eventually to be dominant, in any finite period of time the possibility always remains that his predictions have not yet had time to work themselves out. The only really firm prediction he makes is the eventual triumph of socialism. On the world scene, the number of Marxist-oriented socialist nations certainly have expanded. Nevertheless, it is impossible to apply this as a test because of the programmatic nature of Marxism. It is because of Marx that socialism has developed, or is it the result of the forces Marx analyzed that Socialist nations have appeared on the world scene? Are there other reasons? Certainly we have no opportunity for a critical experiment here.

Despite this negative result some progress is made in Chapter I in identifying the dialectic as a scientifically inadmissible way of making predictions, and in setting up criteria for the meaningfulness of terms. It is then possible to examine the basic theoretical variable of Marx's political economy—value. We examine its credentials, so to speak, in Chapter II. Insofar as it depends on the dialectical materialism rather than empirical evidence we can safely dismiss it. But we must carefully consider the possibility that there are scientific grounds for the labor theory of value.

The possibility remains that Marx's exploitation theory based on the labor theory of value might still be acceptable and might be justified on grounds logically independent of dialectical materialism. Marx thought that this was the case and that he had shown how exploitation occurred under capitalism. I seek to prove that unless Marx makes unwarranted and unduly restrictive assumptions, he cannot hold to a materialistic labor value. He must inevitably be pushed in the direction of multiple factor, subjective cost theories. In the end Marx must rely on subjective demand schedules in order to explain the facts of exchange of commodities. Since the labor theory of value cannot be independently established, Marx cannot use labor value as a verification of his system of dialectical deductions.

In Chapter III we examine Marx's application of the value theory to the wage bargain. We see that he becomes further committed to subjective considerations. Further, his conclusions are shown to be in contradiction with the facts of continued existence of profit and the apparent decreasing misery of the proletariat. Marx interprets this as a contradiction within capitalism itself rather than in his system and goes on to develop a theory of progressively worsening business cycles. We must follow him here and demonstrate how this theory depends on his metaphysical value theory. Particularly in this field there are valuable hints taken up by later economists; but the prediction of the economic breakup of capitalism in a violent depression or secular stagnation or both is not substantiated.

In the final chapter we examine post-Marxist economics. One

view is represented by Lenin who seeks to show how capitalism in its imperialist phase will destroy itself, and sets the corresponding tactical course for the proletarian. The other Revisionist approach is less identified with one writer, although the beginning of this train of thought is associated with Eduard Bernstein. This view would credit Marx with being an unusually perceptive economist and humanitarian who raised many of the key issues and problems of our economy and who led the social protest against the shocking conditions of the working class. They draw their inspiration from this element of Marxism, but agree with the thesis of this book that Marx has been unable to prove that the problems of capitalism are, in principle, insoluble. Revisionism addresses itself to the solution of the problems and leaves the question of socialism open as a possible, but not necessarily the only or the best, means to that end.

MURRAY WOLFSON

December, 1965

Acknowledgments

My first stirring intimation that the fundamental methodological rather than merely formal economic considerations were amiss in Marxian economics goes back to 1950, when I was completing my graduate residence at the University of Wisconsin under the direction of Professor James S. Earley. He suggested that I work with Professor Julius Weinberg, whose Socratic questioning always served to lead to the essential issues. My obligation to both these teachers is more than intellectual. I have an unfulfillable personal debt to their kindness and example.

This book could not have been written but for the advice, criticism, and friendship of Professor Eugene Rotwein then of the University of Wisconsin and now of Queens College, New York. I hope this book reflects his insistence on realism and relevance in economic theorizing.

Needless to say, none of these three people necessarily agrees with the conclusions I have reached. Indeed my greatest debt is to them for their teaching of the Wisconsin tradition of independent "winnowing and sifting" of ideas in search of the truth.

I have also benefited greatly from the constructive criticism of Professor Peter J. D. Wiles of the London School of Economics and from the advice and encouragement of Professor Martin Bronfenbrenner of the Carnegie Institute of Technology.

I am also greatly indebted to Professor Charles B. Friday and the other members of the economics department of Oregon State University for their encouragement and for comments on this manuscript in its various stages of completion. My thanks also go to the Oregon State University Graduate Research Council for generous financial support of my research.

My wife, Betty, has always been the inspiration for all my positive efforts. If this book is one of them, its completion is the result of her affection and understanding—not to speak of forbearance.

Contents

List of Tables

A Reappraisal of Marxian Economics

Introduction

Good sense is of all things in the world the most equally distributed,
for everybody thinks himself so abundantly provided with it, that
even those most difficult to please in all other matters do not com-
monly desire more of it than they already possess. It is unlikely that
this is an error on their part; it seems rather to be evidence in support of the view that the power of forming a good judgment and of
distinguishing the true from the false, which is properly speaking
what is called Good Sense or Reason, is by nature equal in all men.
Hence too, it will show that the diversity of our opinions does not
proceed from some men being more rational than others, but solely
from the fact that our thoughts pass through diverse channels and
the same objects are not considered by all. For to be possessed of
good mental powers is not sufficient; the principal matter is to apply them well. The greatest minds are capable of the greatest vices
as well as of the greatest virtues, and those who proceed very slowly
may, provided they always follow the straight road, really advance
much faster than those who, though they run, forsake it.

Descartes[1]

It appears that I must present the reader with a discussion of
not one but two methods: my own and that of Karl Marx. Methodological investigations are usually best read after the substan-
tive arguments have been elaborated. This is true even though
method may be logically prior to the rest of the argument. Consequently, unless the reader is familiar with ground traversed in
this book, I would suggest a rereading of this Introduction after
he has gone through the first three chapters.

Marx's method is another matter. Marxism cannot be evaluated
adequately unless the methodological expression of his dialectical

materialist philosophy is constantly borne in mind. Although Veblen saw this sixty years ago, it has become necessary to restate the case.[2]

A critical analysis of Marxian economics may employ two different methods. The first alternative would be to discuss the fact that Marx and his followers held certain views; the second would attempt an analysis of the factual and logical content of the Marxist view itself. These methods are both fruitful and in practice may be complementary. A review of the evolution of Marxian thinking and its dependence on antecedent ideologies may be a useful heuristic device to state the issues for analysis. Analysis can, in turn, throw much light on the logical considerations which influenced Marx and his followers to adopt certain positions. Nevertheless, much confusion arises from a failure by too many writers to keep the methods conceptually distinct.[3]

The first approach method is usually historical although the explanations of the reasons for Marx arriving at certain conclusions may also be psychological or sociological.[4] Employing the methods of the behavioral disciplines, one might make careful explication of the distinction between the work of Marx and Engels, trace the development of their doctrine, describe their collaboration, and relate their activities to the events in Europe in the last century. George Lichtheim has written a heavily documented and widely read book of this type.[5]

A difficulty inherent in this method is the need to settle accounts with the validity of the Marxian theory. Since historiography must have at least an implicit theoretical vantage point and since Marxism is an historical doctrine, a judgment regarding the content of the theory persistently tends to obtrude into the factual statements of Marx's activities.

The difficulty is not logically insurmountable. It is no more necessary to argue the merits of the Marxian system in order to study it fruitfully in the first sense, than it is required to engage in petrifying theological debate in order to discuss the history of Christianity and its place in the affairs of men. Insight may certainly be obtained by this method into the urgent policy questions of relation between nations or political and social groups within nations when some of them are influenced by Marxism.

It is not necessary to assume Lichtheim's extreme position that Marxism must be of no significance in current affairs in order for us to be able to carry out such an analysis. Clearly if Marxism must have no further influence on world politics before one may write about it then Lichtheim's book is premature to say the least.[6] Only in the sense that it is psychologically difficult, but not impossible, to make such an analysis is there justification for his quotation of Hegel's dictum that wisdom as represented by the owl of Minerva flies out only at the dusk of a historical day of the *Weltgeist*.[7]

The study of Marxism in the second sense is still a pressing problem. Pragmatically, the widespread acceptance of Marxism in both the communist world and the uncommitted sector of mankind imposes upon those who are critical of this development the responsibility of engaging in intellectual debate. This "ideological warfare," in the true sense of the word, is infinitely preferable to military or psychological warfare, which coerces rather than convinces.

Furthermore, the sticky fact remains that the owl of Minerva has not flown out. It is to Marx's credit that the economic issues he raised are still the real problems of mature capitalism, even if he did not succeed in showing that they are insurmountable within the confines of bourgeois society. If one is to argue that even a modified capitalism is a viable social order, it is necessary to examine the argument he advanced.

We may isolate four questions raised by Marx which I will state in the form in which they are discussed today: (a) Can there be full employment and high real wages without at the same time eliminating the profit incentive? (b) Can depressions be controlled and a reasonable degree of full employment maintained along with control of inflation? (c) Can the concentration of economic power be controlled and the public protected from the economic and political evils of monopoly? (d) Can the developed nations assist the other areas of the world to progress economically, or must the relationship be one of colonialism and exploitation?

I submit that unless the social scientist has agonized over these issues he has failed to deal with the realities of our time. Yet these are precisely the issues which Marx raised a century ago: (a) the theory of the reserve army of unemployed and the subsistence theory of wages; (b) the theory of the "decennial cycle" and the tendency of the rate of profit to fall; (c) the concentration and centralization of capital; and, (d) the theory of imperialism which was actually elaborated by the followers of Marx, but which closely follows the lead of the original.

Is Marx right? This is the question which the present analysis attempts to answer. But once having posed the question in the present tense, the method of arriving at an answer is not obvious. Certainly few would deny that Marx was partly right. Marx was a pioneer in pointing realistically to areas of conflict of interest to replace the fiction of a social contract among basically compatible individuals as the keystone of political structure. Marx anticipated much of later sociology when he identified group and class conditioning as important factors in explaining individual behavior. We could extend this list of contributions to impressive length. Most serious non-Marxist economists have reacted to Marx being partly right by adopting an eclectic approach. These writers have tended particularly to separate the economic and philosophical aspects of his work. This method has not been without success. By being able to pick and choose among the numerous innovations in technique suggested in the Marxist literature, economic scholarship has been able to add to its own theoretical armament.[8] In fact, some have argued that Marx's economics and his philosophy of history are logically independent of each other and not only can be but ought to be evaluated separately.[9]

The drawback of this approach is that it is not responsive to the urgent question which Marxism presents to the world today: Is the Sino-Soviet revolution an example for the aspiration of mankind for a better life? It is in this sense that we must judge Marx right or wrong. In answering in the affirmative Marxists invoke not only economics but also the philosophical concept of historical necessity. In speaking of historical changes in one country, Marx says to others:

De te fabula narratur. Intrinsically . . . it is a question of these laws themselves, of these tendencies working with iron necessity toward inevitable results. The country that is developed industrially only shows to the less developed the image of its future.[10]

Economic reasoning, if it is to judge whether Marx is right, should arrive at a statement whether his prediction of the inevitable collapse of capitalism and its replacement by socialism is justified. It is a thesis of this essay that this judgment cannot be accomplished without an analysis of the philosophical preconceptions. Marx's dialectical materialism is—as the defenders of Marx have noted—both a justification of and a precondition for understanding his theory of value and through it most of the rest of the specifically economic analysis. To be sure, some of Marx's economic insights can be used without the philosophy. Nevertheless, I hope that it will become evident that theory of value is the central economic proposition from which the inevitability of the change of the social order is deduced. If Marx is not right in the sense I have suggested, then accounts must be settled with the philosophical justification for his economics.

A complete philosophical discussion of dialectical materialism is not only beyond my field of specialization but would result in a volume of unmanageable length. Consequently, I must content myself to leave the detailed philosophical criticism to others, and sketch the outline of the issues involved so that I may show their relation to economic theory.

Although Marx is not right, he might still be only wrong with respect to the details of his formal economic theorizing. One might be able to bring Marx up to date. I do not propose to pick at the minor flaws in a sweeping theoretical structure which might be rectified. To do that would neither serve my purpose in evaluating Marxism nor do justice to his argument. However, some Marxists have concluded that to patch up the weaknesses of Marx's century-old economics requires the adoption of the more drastic remedy of dispensing with the labor theory of value. This revision has been advocated for many years by Oskar Lange.[11] The argument from the alleged logical independence of the philosophy and economics of Marx is the converse of the proposition of the non-Marxian eclectic. Just as the fundamental economic outlook cannot be defended without recourse to philosophical argument, I think it can be shown that the philosophy of history is not capable of standing alone. It is not enough to argue, as Lange does in a number of places, that socialism "works" or that it may be desirable according to his criteria. It has to be shown how capitalism *has* to decline before the new social order if the philosophy of history is to be operational. This is a problem for economic analysis. While it is possible that some new economic analysis might replace the orthodox Marxian one, thus far none seems to be forthcoming. Eliminating labor as the source of value in Marxism would not repair but emasculate the notion of historical necessity.

A more orthodox Marxian view is represented by the outstanding Marxian economist Maurice Dobb. He argues that the labor theory of value is wrong because every theory is only approximately true and hence also partly wrong. Dobb accepts the crudities of the labor theory of value as only a first approximation to price phenomena. But he retains this theory as a justifiable abstraction which is necessary to support the revolutionary historical conclusions of the philosophy.[12] The philosophy, in turn, prescribes the method which arrives at the labor theory of value and all its consequences.

We must then examine the labor theory of value and Marx's economics for: (1) its internal consistency; (2) its coincidence with the facts at least to the point of not being contradicted by the phenomena it purports to explain; (3) the degree to which it actually does make meaningful, testable statements about the facts of experience; and, (4) the way in which it both supports and is supported by the rest of the Marxian edifice.

Let us start afresh and examine his system as a whole. We ask ourselves, first, what did Marx intend to prove? Then, in discussing how he went about proving it, we make his philosophical preconceptions explicit. In this way we hope to arrive at a more fundamental criticism of his economics. We examine how his economics contributed to his conclusions about the course of history. As a by-product of this procedure we may make some contribution to bridging the communication gap between Marxist and non-Marxist economists. Behind the semantic problems the difficulty arises from frequently unexpressed preconceptions of the nature and tasks of a scientific explanation of social phenomena.

Now if we are going to critically examine the content of Marxism for the twentieth century, this can most profitably be done in terms of the more highly developed tools of economic analysis of this century. It makes little practical difference to us now that Marx might have survived earlier criticism. Consequently, we must restate the original formulation in terms which are more amenable to our analysis. Where this is done I have resorted to extensive quotation from Marx in order to show that there has been no distortion of his position. Where ambiguous interpretations of what Marx meant arise, I have attempted to choose the alternative that is most consonant with the body of the Marxian system. We must present Marxism in its strongest, most consistent posture, to present a useful critique for our time.

I am interested in Marxism rather than the historical Marx. Yet I believe this approach results in a more faithful account of the spirit of his writings than the antiquarian quotation-chopping that is now the fashion. It is his underlying internal consistency between economic theory and philosophical materialism that permits us to make an over-all judgment of his system and policy proposals. For these reasons I feel the most fruitful studies of Marxism are not eclectic; they either accept or reject the whole structure.

Much of the misinterpretation of Marx results from a separate, piecemeal approach. For instance, in recent years intensive research in Marx's early writings and unfinished manuscripts has convinced some Western historians that Marx's economics and materialist philosophy were logically separate and that the "real" Marx was interested in neither. The unpublished fragments were discovered in 1932 and have only recently become available in English.[13] These writings by the young Marx represent an intermediate phase between the Feuerbachian restatement of Rousseau's humanism as a radical critique of Hegel and the materialism of the mature Marx. Like Rousseau and Feuerbach, Marx attempts to use man as the object of analysis rather than class. Consequently, it is humanness which is lost (alienated) in capitalist society and which man seeks to regain by a communist utopia. Man's "species-nature" is by definition not an alterable or evolving classification; consequently, the changes that Marx advocates in this early draft of his radical thought bear a volitional character. Man is not bound by necessity, historical or otherwise, in these writings. It is easy to see that there is a relation between this view and the contemporary existentialist longings to regain individual human meaning in a collectivized world by artistic or religious expressions of spirit.[14]

The conclusion that has been drawn by some is that it was Engels rather than Marx who was the materialist. We cannot deny that Engels did most of the specifically philosophical writing in their collaboration and mutual criticism.[15] Nevertheless, it seems absurd to inflict a view on Marx which he not only refused to publish but which is at variance with his well-known specific philosophical utterances. Materialism is the core of Marxism. It is the device with which Marx combats his own earlier notion that social change develops by contrast with "what is" and "what ought to be." For Marx the contrast is between "what is" and "what is becoming." Man's notions of "what ought to be" are seen by him as the consequence of the material, deterministic, objective logic of history.[16]

All this confusion could be avoided if adequate attention had been paid to the economic theory that accompanied Marx's philosophy. I think it is evident that the labor theory of value in its Marxian form is the result of the search for a materialist basis for exchange.[17] Unlike some of the writing of Adam Smith, labor for Marx is a material expenditure of effort not the endurance of subjective pain, disutility of effort, or "toil and trouble" of work. Similarly, the positive satisfaction of goods is of no significance in value determination. By the time he writes of the "fetishism of commodities" he acts as if it is utterly meaningless to talk about utility as a universal category which has intensive magnitudes to an individual. Usefulness is a particular material property of the physical object, so that subjective "humaneness" is not quantifiable in terms of satisfactions or dissatisfactions. The really significant aspect of the 1844 document is that the economics which accompanies the humanistic philosophy not only is immature Marxian economics but is greatly influenced by that aspect of Smith's labor theory of value that spoke of toil and trouble rather than material effort. Marx specifically rejects this subjective aspect of Smith's theory of value by the time he writes *Capital* as the economic aspect of his turn to materialism. In both cases the philosophy and the economics are consistent with one another. The alienation of labor in the mature Marx is not so much the loss of a metaphysical human species-nature but the loss of surplus value to the capitalist and the impoverishment of the worker. Marx then goes on to portray the degradation and loss of human dignity that accompanies exploitation in this materialist sense.

I · Method

While the materialist interpretation of history points out how social development goes on—by a class struggle that proceeds from maladjustment between economic structure and economic function—it is nowhere pointed out what is the operative force at work in the process. It denies that human discretion and effort seeking a better adjustment can furnish such a force, since it makes man the creature of circumstances. . . . The materialistic theory conceives of man as exclusively a social being, who counts in the process solely as a medium for the transmission and expression of social laws and changes; whereas he is, in fact, an individual, acting out his own life as such.[1]

Thorstein Veblen

What did Marx Intend to Prove?

Firstly, Marx wanted to show that capitalism must destroy itself. The destructive forces arise from within the system itself and operate through the proletariat as a class of nonowners of means of production. This class, Marx argued, would be driven to social revolution by the inability of a capitalist-directed economy to continue to produce. Marx declined to be more specific as to the circumstances of this breakdown, and speculation on this issue has aroused no little controversy among his followers.[2] Nevertheless, without spelling out events to come, Marx foresaw as inevitable circumstances under which capitalism would not be able to function at anywhere near full employment; or, the conditions of the working class would degenerate so seriously as to make it impossible for them to continue to live in the old way.

Secondly, the death of capitalism was absolutely inevitable.

The conclusion of a necessary social revolution could be deducted apodictically from the science of society that Marx was to create. Scientific socialism could demonstrate the moribund nature of capitalism to even the most reluctant listener. It followed that those who remained unconvinced were to be viewed as one or another variety of knaves or fools. In the first instance the knaves (particularly the "vulgar economists") were the hypocritical apologists for capitalism. In the second alternative they were the, as yet, uneducated masses awaiting enlightenment. The only remaining possibility was that certain elements of society, the petty bourgeoisie, might have an ambivalent class position. Hence they might vacillate in allegiance between the revolutionary proletariat at one time and the reactionary bourgeoisie at another.

Thirdly, the institutions of the economy (indeed all of the social superstructure) are derivatives of the basic economic conflict between antiquated modes of ownership and social organization for production on one hand and the development of productive technique and equipment on the other. Institutional forms are the ideological products of the most real material essence which holds society together, that is, productive relations in the manufacture of goods. Much effort is wasted by scholars in the study of the superstructure of society when they treat it as if it had an independent development of its own. In reality its evolution is determined by the more fundamental economic relations which lead to the replacement of one superficial social integument by another more appropriate to the prevailing mode of production. It follows that such notions as democratic political systems, culture and the arts, and science itself cannot be evaluated as ends in themselves, but are of significance only as they facilitate or hinder the new social order. The standard of judgment in valuing any human activity is its impact on the proletarian revolution to come.

Fourthly, the individual is realistically treated as fundamentally an agent of his economic class. Obviously, since his views and desires are subjective, as opposed to the material interests of the group, it is the class which is historically destined to perform the revolutionary role. The individual is significant only as he takes part in the group movement. Outside the class context he counts for little in originating social change. For Marx, means and ends representing individual attitudes coalesce into the objective inevitability of the class revolution. The individual who opposes or anticipates the inevitable march of history toward socialism will be reduced to impotence by the train of events no matter how outstanding a person he may be. Conversely, the press of the social struggle will spontaneously bring forward outstanding persons to provide the leadership. The individual, then, can find fulfillment only if he is part of the wave of the future.

This viewpoint permits of enormous discipline and self-sacrifice for the cause. The utter conviction of inevitable triumph and the identification with the liberation of oppressed mankind produces Lenin's "professional revolutionary," who, with the zeal of the Christian martyr, can spend a lifetime underground and still, at the key moment, provide the organizational spark that ignites the flame of revolution. The more reasonable view of social change suggested by Bernstein is that the goal of the socially minded individual should be the improvement of the lot of the ordinary person and that socialism may or may not be a means to that end depending on how successfully capitalism is able to solve its problems. Socialism could not properly be an end in itself, unless it could be proved that the breakdown of capitalism is inevitable; then the least social hardship would be entailed in adopting the policy of getting the unpleasant business of dispatching it over with as quickly as possible.

Rationalism and the Background of Marx's View of Science

The unifying attribute of Marxism is the belief that it is a body of scientific deductions from the laws of motion of society.

It is this which gives "scientific socialism" its characteristic militant policy and makes it impatient of reformist change. Reform is at best a preparation for revolution and at worst a palliative and a diversion from it. Marxist theorists like Dobb and Sweezy wish to hold fast to this revolutionary practical application to political program. In order to evaluate this train of thought it is therefore necessary for us to digress from a specifically economic argument and examine what Marx meant by scientific explanation. It will be seen that his view differs markedly from the concept which appears in a fair number of writings on the subject.[3]

Scientific explanation in our usage, while it has not been without controversy and difficulties, ultimately rests on the argument of the British empiricists—Locke, Berkeley, and Hume. The logical formulation of their view is that there can be no logically necessary connection between statements of fact. Such connection refers only to relations between propositions or between propositions and statements of fact. For example, we might argue with logical necessity that, from the propositions, "If it rains today, it will rain tomorrow," and "If it rains tomorrow, it will rain the day following," therefore "If it rains today, it will rain the day after tomorrow." Or we might assert the classical categorical syllogism, "All men are mortal" (proposition), "Socrates is a man" (fact), therefore "Socrates is mortal" (fact). It is impossible to deny the conclusions of the deductions and still assert the first two terms without self-contradiction. There is no such relation between matters of fact. It is perfectly possible to deny the consequent of a statement relating two facts in a hypothetical statement without contradicting the antecedent. Thus we can certainly deny that Socrates is a man without denying that he (she) exists at all.

It follows that it is impossible to deduce matters of fact from any sort of reasoning process which does not at the outset contain factual statements. All meaningful statements must be about propositions, must be shown to be about experience, or must be an analytic series of equivalent expressions. This idea has been variously expressed as Locke's insistence on knowledge arising from the "simple ideas" of sense after his denial of "innate ideas," Hume's tracing of knowledge to impression of sense, Carnap's "protocol statements" or Popper's "basic statements." Empiricism led science's battle to free itself from Aristotelian formal or final causes expressing a supersensible essence or purpose of objects from which their properties might be deduced. To the empiricists, essences were nominal, verbal summaries of accumulated sense experience with classes of objects and followed from experience rather than preceding it. Individual writers made valiant attempts to reconcile this view with preconceptions transcending experience such as belief in God, matter, substance. Hume, however, relentlessly pressed to the conclusion that these entities were neither experienced nor implied by any aspect of experience, and he unceremoniously consigned both materialism and religion to the flames.

Empiricist scientific explanation, unlike Marxism does not attempt to look for absolute, certain truth since such certainty is only available in connecting propositions according to verbal or symbolic rules of manipulation. What, then, is the place of the causal relationship which plays such a prominent role in the development of science? The causation itself is not sensuously observable. Hume's explanation was that it is human nature that connects events after they have been conjoined in experience in the past. Human psychology is such that a feeling is aroused that event A will be succeeded by event B in the future if it has done so repeatedly in the past. There is no logical warrant for this expectation; the psychological connection is all that can properly be called cause.

Popper amends this and describes causality as a methodological convention. It is useful in scientific discourse to state factual, and hence contingent statements as propositions, that is, as if they were universally true. In the absence of any possible way of knowing about future events with certainty we find it useful to be guided by the past assuming provisionally that the future will behave as the past has. We make generalizations based upon past experience; but since 100 percent induction is a trivial and useless procedure for prediction, our general laws retain their contingent character. We therefore adopt the further methodological device of continually submitting our conclusions to test by experience. Furthermore, we extend this notion of testing of causal inference to all theoretical variables which we cannot observe directly. Thus such words as mass, electron, and value in scientific discourse can be meaningfully used only as we can show them to be terms in causal laws that both have empirically testable consequences and are required to explain the observed facts.

Empirical meaning is given to unobserved terms by placing them as elements in a deductive system or calculus, which starts from them as premises and which combines with analytic statements and causal proposition to predict fact. By comparing deduction with observation the system is subject to test. It will not do to simply verify such a system since a conclusion consistent with one hypothesis, or system of hypotheses, can also be consistent with others. What is required is to state the system so that it has potential falsifiers—events which, if they occurred, would require us to reject the theory as a universal statement. A theory with no falsifiers is metaphysical in Popper's sense of the word. It lies beyond empirical meanings.

A theory with more possible falsifiers, is more meaningful since it has been subject to more thorough testing. Consequently an hypothesis which is part of a wider deductive system is subject to test at a multitude of points, while a "rule of thumb" has only slight claims to reliability. An overdetermined system, one with more hypotheses than are needed to explain the observable facts, is not in testable form since, if it succeeds its tests, it is impossible to determine which of the hypotheses has been vindicated and which might still be false. Marx's concept of value is, I believe, such a metaphysical concept, since it is superfluous for the explanation of the price ratios of exchange of commodities. These are determined, as Marx knew, by the historically evolved attitudes of buyers and sellers of goods and factors of production. Indeed, according to Marx, "value" itself is an unobservable substratum underlying the price at which goods are sold on the market. Why, then, does Marx bother with the concept at all?

The justification which Marx advances for value as a necessary economic variable involves its place in the dialectical explanation of history. This requires that we must understand what Marx meant by dialectical scientific explanation.

Marx's attitude toward the requirements of a science arose out of the rationalist philosophy of the Enlightenment as it appeared on the Continent. To the rationalist empirical scientific explanation is no explanation at all. To be sure, the progress of rationalist philosophy involved the rejection of the Aristotelian final causes (Spinoza). It expunged the problem of "for what purpose" from the requirements for a satisfactory explanation of natural events. But rationalism recoils from the empiricist answer to the question, "Why does an event occur?" The reason given by empiricism is: "Because it has done so in the past, and, without really being sure we are justified, we have a feeling that it is likely to do so in the future." The rationalist argues that he has been told nothing at all. He wants to know why an event *had to* occur. Why was it necessary? What is the necessary connection between cause and effect? If there is to be any science at all it must provide him with propositions which are universally and certainly true, not mere generalizations.

In terms of their preoccupation with the physical sciences of their day the rationalists seemed not without justification in their demand. The empiricists (with the possible exception of Berkeley) had been mainly interested in the social ("moral") sciences. They were interested in using their skepticism against religious and political dogmatism: if no one could be certain that he had the ultimate truth then the most sensible social organization should leave room for doubt and minority dissent. But to some

natural scientists of the Newtonian age the progress of knowledge of our physical environment appeared as the logical deducing of rigorously demonstrable conclusions about matters of
fact from universally true, a priori self-evident axioms. The apparent universal truth of the premises of geometry and mechanics
seemed to preclude the possibility of their being inductively derived from experience. It is significant that Locke and Hume
were prepared to consign all nonempirical statements to the
flames except for mathematics. Of course, many years later with
the advance of non-Euclidean geometry it became manifest that
strides of Descartes (analytic geometry) and Leibniz (calculus)
and their colleagues were really useful deductive systems rather
than factual statements about the real world. But from the rationalist vantage point it seemed as if they had simply excogitated
ultimate truth about space, time, and the movement of rigid
bodies. It seemed, further, that they had arrived at a *more real*
understanding of the universe than could be obtained from mere
observation. The objects of sense included such "secondary qualities" (Locke) as color, odor, and the like, which were thought
to be derivative of the reality of mass, distance, and time and
their relationships. Ultimate reality can be discovered by logical
demonstration—sensation deals only in contingent sequences.

Not only was sensation inadequate, but it was notoriously fal-
lible. Pure reason was above the errors inherent in human sense
perception. Scientific explanation, Spinoza argued, could avoid
error by integrating all hitherto isolated Aristotelian faculties into
a single deductive system. The main shafts of rationalist argument were part of the war of science against the fetters of scholasticism. But while they were as much part of the Enlightenment
as the liberal English empiricism was, they approached it from
the point of view of system builders rather than the skeptic.

Despite the success of the rationalists, singular factual data
stubbornly refused to be deduced from their system. Science, it
was true, was integrating propositions into an increasingly more
universal edifice of knowledge, but these remain only the major

premise of the categorical syllogism which might predict events.
Even if the propositions were accepted as beyond doubt, the
singular data of experience must be exogenously introduced as
initial conditions so that the principles might be applied. This
is true in any set of propositions, whether empirical or a priori
in origin.

The more ingenious the attempts of rationalist philosophers to
account for contingent events were, the more fantastic the speculations became. The occasionalism of Descartes' followers made
God appear as a *deus ex machina* which, by a recurring miracle
at every instant, recreated the world and assured its consistency
with natural law; Spinoza reduced the singular objects to a
universal substance which contained all logically consistent attributes "in it," but he could not explain how singular events
could be derived from an undifferentiated universal; Leibniz,
taking the opposite tack, attempted to include the whole universe in the predicates of an infinite number of singular atomic
"monads."

While Marx recognized the fantastic nature of the rationalist
solutions, he agreed with the demand for causal explanation in
terms of some sort of monistic universal. In spite of his apprecia-
tion of the blows empiricism struck against scholasticism, Marx
felt that it was a shortsighted, narrow philosophy. The unwilling-
ness of these critics to penetrate to underlying material reality,
he argued, was a reflection of the narrow pragmatism of the
British bourgeoisie. Hume was a "shamefaced materialist" according to Engels, while the rationalists were the early dialec-
ticians even though they were infected with idealism.[4]

The rationalist solution to the problem of the causal relationship between mind and body directly influenced the Marxian
view of social development. Descartes had posited a division between the essences of thought and body (extension) which were
reunited by the divine guarantee. That perception would accu-
rately reflect the external world, the solution to the mind-body
problem which was carried on in later rationalist thought, be-

comes the rudiments of a theory of human behavior. The same ultimate explanation which imposed the laws of reason on matter also was made to apply with equal determinacy to the thoughts of man. Spinoza emphasized that what appear as voluntary acts of man were the determinate logical consequences of the attributes of God. Marx substituted Matter for the deity as the rationalist ultimate.

Now to empiricism all experience was equal in contingent status. Consequently, ideas and impressions which appear to come from the influence of material objects on us are no more fundamental than those which are of obvious subjective "ideological" origin such as tradition, volition, morality, religion, and the like. An empiricist social science would look to connections beween social events and would weigh the economic and the ideological as factors in predicting events. The weights would depend on a testable theory of experience in which the importance of economic and other facts would be considered. A priori, Marx decided upon economic motivations as part of the materialist conception of history. In his hands materialism becomes the materialist conception of exchange value and the theory of the class struggle.[5]

Dialectical Rationalism—The Roots of the Marxist Method

With Hume and Leibniz, philosophy was at an impasse. Rationalism had entangled itself in a mesh of metaphysical absurdities which brought the ridicule of men of good sense such as Voltaire. Yet Leibniz had effectively challenged empiricism by denying the meaningfulness of Locke's "simple idea." Can one simply receive data without conceptualizing it, working it up into some sort of system however crude it may be? What is an object of thought? A thing? But this very selection and synthesis of undigested sense data into things implies a theory of solid, coherent bodies, and a Galilean theory of time and space. Is the object a collection of qualities like round, smooth, solid? This conception implies a logically prior classification of the meaning of these terms; criteria must be established to demarcate the round from the square. Although the classification may be suggested from experience and indeed be an abstraction from it as Locke suggested, yet the very selection of the aspects of experience by our consciousness requires an a priori notion of the way in which the manifold materials of experiences are connected. That is to say, we logically require a theory of organization of experience to make any observations at all.

Kant seized on this point to reconcile the two strands of the philosophy of science. His "Copernican revolution" consisted of finding the a priori universals in us, not either in the deity or in experience. The laws of space and time (Euclidean geometry and the mathematics of counting) are logically prior to experience, said Kant. Yet they are statements of fact (a priori synthetic), because the human mind is so constructed that it thinks in spatial and temporal terms. There is no way in which reason may know whether things in themselves are "in" space and time. But for scientific purposes this is irrelevant. The conclusions of geometry and arithmetic are universally and therefore necessarily true of all experience since we must synthesize the manifold facts of experience. In other words these a priori synthetic universals are constitutive of experience which must therefore conform to their laws.

Kant expanded this idea to include other necessary connections which the human mind had to make between events on the basis of experience, for example, cause and effect and the notion of the objective thing and its predicates. He showed how such synthetic constitutive categories are a priori and are observed in their pure nonempirical form in the categories of formal Aristotelian logic. By explaining the demand for universal necessity as a human metaphysical tendency, Kant preserved the use of necessity in discourse concerning propositions about scientific matters. At the same time as he accepted the search for universal statements as a methodology of science, he blocked the extension of universals derived from experience to any ultimate ontology which transcended any test by experience. The search for the "unconditioned" was the result of the human *psychological* necessity of thinking in causal chains, but causality only applied to sense experiences. Attempts to deduce matters of fact beyond sense experience only ended in self-contradiction, the antinomies of pure reason. For instance, one could argue that the universe had to have a beginning because an infinite time would have elapsed until the present. This is impossible by definition of infinite as not finite. All the same, each moment in time has a preceding one so that the universe must be an infinite regress in time. Reason, says Kant, has no warrant to answer such questions which transcend experience. The same basic critique applies to attempts to prove the existence of God, Matter, Monads, and the like.

Kant has been shown to be wrong in his estimate of the a priori universality of his ideas of space, time, and logic. All three are not absolute categories of human experience but have undergone change since Kant's day. The most striking change is the discovery that Euclidean geometry is only one of many possible geometries. Furthermore some of the non-Euclidean systems turn out to have physical significance. The self-evident axioms of Euclidean geometry are now seen to have a dual nature: on one hand they are an empirical theory which is approximately true of objects of moderate size and velocity; on the other, they are stated in the form of a series of universal propositions from which deductions can be made. The deductions are necessary consequences of the axioms; but their applicability to the facts is only as accurate as the axioms themselves in describing experience through the ability of deductions from them to withstand test. Likewise, the Aristotelian logic of subject and predicate has also been amended in harmony with the needs of modern science in the development of symbolic logic. Aristotelian logic seems now to be the formal aspect of Newtonian corpuscular physics as it was present in embryo to the common sense of classical philosophers.

Despite this, the main point that Kant insisted on still remains crucial for the social scientist as an amendment to radical empiricism.[6] The facts do not and cannot speak for themselves. At least a *tentative* theory is required to put data together as we receive it. To be sure the theory is provisional and not absolute, as Kant thought. It must therefore be stated in such a way as to present the logic of the theory, as well as its statements of fact, to test.[7] In no field is the relative a priori nature of theory as critical as in the social sciences. The myriad events in the social manifold elevates methodological considerations above their importance in physical sciences. One is only able to observe the social facts in connection with the theory one holds. Without theory social science degenerates into a kaleidoscope of *ad hoc* observations, inconsistent generalizations and rules of thumb.

While our observations of the past are conditioned by our theory they are consistent with the constitutive categories of the system. Thus there are endless verifications of, say, the class struggle for the Marxist. The reason is simply that events are selected as significant as they relate to class conflict. They are continually chiding advocates of democracy for spouting meaningless abstractions from what Marxists consider the class reality. One may, for instance, speak of bourgeois democracy, proletarian democracy, classical slave democracy, primitive communist democracy, they argue, but not of popular rule in society construed as an aggregate of individuals. Nevertheless it is not really true that one may more realistically start with the direct observation of individuals which are parts of a whole. They too cannot be analyzed without abstraction from experience.[8] As Kant pointed out the synthesis of singular objects in the understanding also requires an a priori theory; individuals are no more given directly by experience as the social unit than are holistic classes or other institutions. When one begins with individuals and their attitudes, the determinants of their attitudes become a matter which must be stated exogenous to the model. The model consequently gives up its claim to draw conclusions as to the causes of these determinants except insofar as it can be shown that there are "feedback" effects from the dynamic changes within the system upon its determining parameters.

Whether one starts from social wholes or individuals one must show the derivative relationship between individual behavior and the nature of group. There must be a "reduction" of laws at one level of abstraction to those at another level.[9] But let there be no mistake, both approaches require abstraction. The choice of abstraction as to which facts are to be absorbed into the deductive system and which may be safely put aside in social science is frequently a matter of the time dimension which we attach to our analysis. If we are concerned with short-run changes in price then there is little controversy that we may accept attitudes and the distribution of wealth as given. If we want to compare social and economic systems then we must have a larger historical time horizon and the problem of equity of the distribution of income in the long run becomes crucial.[10] Since distribution of income is a price matter of factors of production, it is to the determinants of long-run price—roughly the classical notion of value—to which we must turn our attention. Attitudes then must be considered as variables rather than given. Insofar as these are determined by the conditioning of the individual within the group it is to the "holistic" level of abstraction we must turn. It is not "holism" or abstraction which is at fault, but rather that one forgets that these decisions to abstract are empirically justifiable insofar as the theory leading to the decisions is subject to tests directly or through its consequences. The trap into which Marxism has fallen is in framing its categories that synthesize experience so as to eliminate possible falsifications. What is required is that *at each level* of abstraction of a theory it must predict future events which can falsify the theory. If Marx had said all events are defined as fundamentally explained by the economics of the class struggle modified in only a secondary way by ideological considerations, his theory would be meaningful but false. But Marx's hypothesis cannot be false if the ideological considerations are permitted to account for any deviation from material class interest. If he asserts that there are contrary tendencies and that one is dominant, he must also somehow indicate a time perspective for the preponderant tendency to achieve its result. This is especially urgent when the prediction is also the basis for radical policy proposals which themselves are supposed to be based on the most important of the tendencies.

Marx's dialectics permit him to avoid falsification because each assertion contains not only a thesis but an antithesis. Contradiction is part of the event. This is a very strange sort of logic, for if hypotheses are not falsifiable we dismiss them as meaningless and if they are contradicted by events we dismiss them as false. Marx's concept of science however included a new logic derived from Hegel's dialectical universal philosophy.

Now it must be admitted that we have opened the door to the dialectic by pointing out that logic is a verbal calculus adapted to our way of understanding the world. It is therefore subject to change and development as our knowledge progresses. For instance, probability and statistical views of causation in physics introduce new problems in logical analysis. But whatever the calculus—dialectic or otherwise—if it fails to put itself to the test by the device of absorbing self-contradiction into its system, it also absorbs the admission of its uselessness. I shall argue that at crucial points in his argument when Marx is driven to contradiction between his analysis and the facts, he uses the dialectic to avoid the falsification to which his system would otherwise be subject.

Dialectics can best be understood as Hegel's response to the Kantian demonstration of the futility of attempting to deduce matters of fact by pure reason alone.[11] Hegel concluded that traditional logic had to be replaced because its static analysis was unequal to the task. What was needed was the logic of the "constructive negative." The dialectical deduction should start from a most universal Idea (thesis). By proving its contradiction with itself (antithesis), Hegel argues that the original universal is mediated by negation. The result (synthesis) of the negation is a less general category, closer to experience. Knowledge is a *process* of the development of the Idea rather than a compilation of experiences. On one hand, knowledge involves the deduction of the objective world through the alienation of the Idea from itself as a result of its own, internal, self-contradictions. Categories are unable to provide knowledge as mere empty boxes and, therefore, the advance of knowledge demands particular events to provide content.[12] On the other hand, reason demands that the particulars be subsumed under general laws. What ensues is the spiral process of the evolution of thought in the alienation of singulars from universals and their reabsorption into further generalizations. Since reality was to be found in ideas, Hegel felt that he was describing knowledge and reality at the same time.

The process is illustrated in Hegel's first deduction. The most universal category that Hegel could think of is Being. The category common to all ideas is that they *are*. Everything *is!* [13] But undifferentiated Being, like undifferentiated substance, is an idea devoid of content. The simple thesis statement is identical with no knowledge, its contradiction—not Being. The synthesis of the contradiction is a new thesis, Becoming. Now patently the notion of time or any sort of continuum is not a logical consequence of the contradiction, but conclusions derived from experience have been introduced by a play on words. The forced and artificial character of the deductions to fit the facts becomes apparent as the reader penetrates into the Hegelian concepts of natural science.

It is significant, however, that we are psychologically moved from one stage of the deduction to the next in many of the triads. This suggests that since the development of the dialectic is not dependent on deductions and is not a theoretical explanation of the contents of our thought, it may be an account of the way we think.[14] The psychological forces driving our thoughts are not contradictions but contraries. These latter are groups of opposing tendencies—there need not be only two—which result in change taking place. They cannot be analyzed a priori, but are matters for the history of science, that is, for empirical observation, generalization, and testing. The dialectic would have it that the essence of an object is its contradiction, which defines its future course of development as a matter of analytic deduction. It is easy to see how the dialectician would identify a contingent statement of psychological causation with a logically necessary deduction.[15] Putting the matter differently, it is perfectly admissible to explain evolutionary change on the basis of many contraries referring to the same object at the same time; but by definition, a contradiction is a pair of statements which cannot at the same time be both true and false of the same object.[16]

Feuerbach and the Early Marxian Critique of Hegel

While the Hegelian theory stressed change, it retained a conservative element in the teleological aspect of the dialectic. The Prussian state represented to Hegel the rational perfection toward which the Idea was progressing. The German radicals, preparing for the revolution of 1848, turned to the materialism of the French Enlightenment of a century earlier for critical ammunition to be used against the philosophical bulwark of the old regime. Led by Feuerbach, who designated himself a materialist, they criticized the idealism of Hegel. Hegel's Being is really the material world of Nature, Feuerbach announced.[17] Insofar as it was possible for Feuerbach to identify the Hegelian Absolute Idea with God, the attack on Hegel amounted to an attack on the established church. In any case the same criticism applied to both. Ideas are the product of Man's consciousness, so that Man is logically and temporally prior to ideas of God or philosophy.

Hegel had it that singular human consciousness is the alienation of the Universal Idea from itself, just as religion presents individual man as the imperfect creature of God's infinite perfection.

Feuerbach used the Hegelian concept of alienation to depict religion as anthropology. The Idea and God are the products of the projection of human nature suitably idealized and hypostatized into an infinite "other" than itself. If God is universal knowledge, power, and love, it is because these are the natural characteristics of Man. Atheism involves overcoming the alienation of the "esoteric psychology" of religion and permits man to realize that he should deify himself and his own nature. One hears Rousseau in all this in both the philosophical theory and the political conclusion that "the voice of the people is the voice of God." In the inverted Hegelian jargon the Absolute Idea reaches its goal when it overcomes all alienations and returns the perfections into itself in Universal Self-Consciousness.

It is important to realize that this view exalts an abstract universal, Man, not individual men.[18] While not quite inventing a "state of nature," Feuerbach must argue for the existence of an innate "species consciousness" to justify such sublime projections from creatures who, as individuals, seem often as not concerned with more mundane, egoistic, and sometimes predatory goals. Man, unlike the brute, is a "species-being" because he is aware of other individuals like himself and identifies his satisfactions with theirs.

Marx's earliest criticism of capitalism in his *Economic and Philosophic Manuscripts of 1844* is an attempt to extend Feuerbach's argument that religion is anthropomorphism to the rest of Hegel's ideology. If the dialectic is the description of the evolution of the thought of Man rather than objective Reason, might one not understand his nature in more than its religious, ethical aspect, by the same "projective technique"? Hegel had argued that the essence of Man is Labor. Man alienates himself by Labor and includes natural objects in the synthesis of production of wealth which is in turn the foundation of such collective human institutions such as the Family and later the State. While for Hegel the category of Labor is represented as an ideal process of the drive of Reason to acquire knowledge, the young Marx sees it as the creative species characteristic of Man which strives to dominate Nature—to make it his own. But instead of the product of labor becoming the work of the collective universal Man, it remains alienated from him in the form of individual private property. Stored up labor in the form of capital becomes the means of the denigration of Man, the laborer, just as religion was said to do by Feuerbach.[19] Man is reduced to a commodity —a factor of production. Labor becomes a torment rather than the means of satisfying the "truly human" being who collectively freely labors with others of his species. Marx at this stage is reading Smith on the division of labor and the loss of the satisfactions of craftsmanship. He is shocked at the rigorous analysis Ricardo presents of the "inhumanity" of the automatic market mechanism in valuing labor. Communism is, for Marx, the return of the alienated Self to Man, just as atheism was for Feuerbach.

But Marx puts the 1844 manuscript away in his desk as he gains experience from practical revolutionary activity. It is one thing for the youthful radical to decry the injustice of capitalism in 1844, but, when he is faced with the practical political problem of changing the world rather than interpreting it, positive knowledge of the way in which these changes are made is paramount. The notion of *species consciousness* which suffices for romantic longings in 1844 is no longer adequate the next year when Marx jots down the famous *Theses on Feuerbach*. The question now is not "What ought or ought not to be" but "What is, and what is becoming."

Feuerbach's species consciousness was advanced as a materialist criticism of Hegel, yet was not a satisfactory substitute to explain social behavior. In what could such an entity inhere? If it is a psychological datum, consciousness as an empirical statement about an individual's thoughts, is in direct opposition to Marx's rationalist notions of scientific explanation. What is it that ultimately causes these thoughts? To explain the ideas by other ideas either implies an infinite regress or a return to Hegel's objective self-subsistent idea.

But suppose there is a meaningful way in which one could talk about human nature? This might be at once empirical fact and also provide the social determinism. Could one compare the consciousness of individuals? Perhaps in defiance of anthropology one might concede that the projection of a good god rather than a demon tells something about ultimate human nature in a qualitative sense; but the quantitative aspects of such an assertion show it to be a useless concept. Interpersonal comparisons of subjective states such as utility of commodities or the disutility of labor's "toil and trouble" yield absurd results when applied to the problem of exchange of commodities.[20] Clearly it is a fact that different people place different subjective valuations on their effort or their goods. The further Marx pushed into economics, the more evident this must have become to him.

By the time he writes *Capital* he is vehement in his denunciation of the utility calculus of Bentham.[21] Not only was human nature nonquantifiable but, as an innate trait it was not subject to human change. Bentham had brought the conservative elements in a theory of human nature to its ultimate conclusion. Human nature might be conceived of as the misanthropism of Hobbes as well as the charitable view of humanity of Rousseau and Feuerbach. It is as easy to identify the egocentric, capitalist, economic man as the inevitable and unchanging unit upon which an individualistic society must be built as it is to identify him as the species being of collective love which might be the basis for communism.

Moreover species consciousness does not answer the question of how to make real society philosophical, that is, in accord with the ideal of love. In the *Theses* Marx is not yet at the point of annunciating the class struggle, but he is aware that the Feuerbachian view ignores the fact that men are the "product of circumstances and upbringing" and therefore the "human essence is no abstraction inherent in each single individual." [22] Rousseau's model of a civil society is an unstratified collection of individuals with fixed natures, when in reality society is made up of "the ensemble of the social relations." [23] Can society be changed by will alone? Marx suddenly sees his earlier thought in a different light. How is it that he feels compelled to change circumstances of upbringing? What must happen so that others will be similarly inclined and the ideas of communism put into practice? The point is that while "men are the products of circumstances . . . circumstances are changed precisely by men . . . the educator must himself be educated." The process appears to be circular unless it is explained in terms of some other universal. "The coincidence of the changing of circumstances and of human activity can only be conceived and rationally understood as revolutionising practice." [24] Marx turns for explanation to a materialism which identifies thought with the practical activity of a material human being rather than the knowledge by the mind of the material world which exists "in itself." [25]

If the material activity of man is subject to change according to ascertainable laws then one may comprehend at once both the changes in upbringing and the desires by individuals to change the conditions of upbringing. Marx is thus brought back to the Hegelian evolutionary approach to human society.[26]

He now concludes that the categories of Hegelian deductions are really the necessary connections between stages in thought by material human beings. The necessity is not provided by logic, but inheres in Matter and material causation. The mind as a material part of material man must obey the same dialectical laws of contradiction and essence that govern matter. One can still understand reality by standing Hegel on his head, but the universal reality is Matter, not species-consciousness. Man is an active, productive creature who expends labor in the form of physical energy in his interaction with his natural environment.

Dialectical Materialism—Marx's Concept of Science

Marx thought that he was returning the revolutionary Hegelian concept of change to science and reality. Instead of Hegel's "forced and outrageous" constructions based on the development of the Idea, Marx argued that the fundamental reality was matter. Matter underwent the necessary evolution which Hegel had suggested, and the mind merely reflected external changes by changed ideas.

To all intents and purposes Marx fully accepted the teachings of science. He inveighed against the vanity of philosophers who attempted, by speculative means, to dictate conclusions to those who were empirically searching for the secrets of matter. The Absolute Idea of Hegel was a fiction—utterly meaningless.

One might have thought Marx to be an empiricist. He was not. The issue turns on the meaning of the word *matter*. As Hume had shown it has no empirical content. Suppose one were to replace the Idea with Matter. There would be no essential difference between the two systems except to make the proper changes for the advancement of science in the interval between their writing and to account for Marx's attempts to restrain himself from excessive flights of fancy.[27] *Mutatis mutandis* the theories are identical since the scientific data are really introduced a posteriori. They can be introduced at will without challenging the system. Marx obtains endless verification by science, but opens no possibility of falsification by test. Materialism was Marx's way of returning to the Hegelian historical rationalism.

While dialectical materialism has no consequences for physical science in that it is really not a logical calculus, it does contain within it a statement about the nature of human beings and the relation between their thoughts and actions. Materialism, like the rationalism of the seventeenth-century speculative philosophers, is an a priori theory which explains social behavior in terms of an objective essence. While materialism is not empirically meaningful, since it is not subject to test, it does retain its constitutive nature. It governs the crucial selection and interpretation of received social data which, in turn, determine the content of social theory.

We may summarize the philosophical preconceptions which Marx used to establish the categories of his Science of Society:

1. Marx like Hegel is convinced that social science must provide an explanation for human events in terms of a single objective universal. Any explanation not reducible to Matter does not deal with underlying reality. At best an eclectic explanation of history in terms of multiple contributing factors is superficial. It is more likely to be misleading in practice and lead to reform rather than revolution.

2. Matter and its relation with its parts (that is, material people and objects) change in a determinate path. This determination is not a static model, as Leibniz suggested, but an evolutionary process. There is a single, fundamental, material law of social development throughout the history of human society because it is based on the evolution of one fundamental material substance. The task of the social scientist is to discover how material relationships control social affairs.

3. Matter evolves in accordance with the logic of the dialectic. Dialectics is therefore a most general law of nature although it makes no predictions as to what particular future events will be. Evolution occurs by means of contradiction. Here Marx takes over the Hegelian confusion between contrary and contradictory, but interprets it materialistically. Matter is subject to contrary tendencies which result in its modification; it is not in stable equilibrium. Marx's notion of so-called contradiction has it that each stage in social development is defined by a *single* contradiction which constitutes its essence or quality. Quantitative changes in the relation of the opposing forces result in a qualitative change into a new essence with its own defining material contradiction. The task of the social scientist is to define the essential

contradiction for each stage of history and to explain other data in terms of it.

4. Ideology is a derivative of matter and must be explained in terms of matter. For Hegel the world of singular events, facts, was made up of the *other* ideas of the Universal Idea produced by the self-negation of the Universal. For Marx, the ideas of objects in the minds of men are the particular reflections of matter; matter is the evolving universal reality. Ideas arise in the mind of man as a result of the contradiction between material man, equipped with a thinking material brain, and material nature. Hegel provided the name of the contradiction between man and nature: it is practical Labor.[28]

The essence of man is labor. As a result of man's practical interaction with nature they are both changed. Man changes his environment and compels nature to do his bidding; at the same time his ideas are successively brought into *correspondence* with nature by the demands of his practical efforts. Marx imagines that he has made matter-in-itself knowable, not by sensation but by equating it with the material activity of material man. However, by defining mind in terms of practical labor instead of thought and sensation, Marx has eliminated mind as a knower and has replaced it with a stream of material events in the brain. These may be determined by matter, but they do not have to be copies of it as Marx thinks. In fact there is no individual thought at all in this system in the sense of an active synthesizing *mental* effort attempting to rationalize sense information about the material world. But this is in plain contradiction to the fact of just such scientific thought; we do actively think about the objective world when we perceive, abstract, and test. We do more than react to a material world. Our knowledge is limited to sense-information, to be sure, but it is thought.

Marx construes this contradiction with fact as a contrary. Instead of recognizing that his theory is incompatible with observation, he argues that the contradiction between individual mate-

rial man and nature in labor changes the human animal into a
social creature who engages in collective production. Ideas are
derived from labor as collective or class ideologies. They are
different from the sum of individual material reactions to nature.
Knowledge is a social phenomenon. Individual thought is only
significant because it is a reaction by a material man to class
interests. The individual's ideas and hence his freedom to act is
important insofar as he recognizes class necessity. Marx has
turned knowledge into its opposite. It has become a materialistic
theory of why *social* ideologies develop. Marx has really aban-
doned the search for an account of the possibility of human
knowledge of the objective world.[29] Here again we see how
rationalism might discover *that* we think, but it cannot originate
the content of what we as individuals do think.

Marx's Theory of History

To Marx man exists in a material relation with Nature. Production changes both man and his material environment. Man
develops his individual talents and his social organization for
production. At the same time his material environment is altered
by his labor with the accumulation of means of production—
improvements in land, buildings, tools, machinery, and the like.[30]

Although Marx recognizes the importance of these material
changes in increasing production, he treats them as increases in
labor productivity. The physical effort of the living material
human being in interacting with things, whether it be land in
the classical sense or means of production produced by man
himself, is the only productive force.[31] As man develops his
mastery over nature he begins to extend his domination over
other men because they are material objects of nature.[32] With
the advance of productive technique it becomes possible to
enslave captives rather than eat them, since they are now able to
produce a surplus product above the requirements for their own
subsistence. Thus with the agricultural and pastoral stages of

production we see the beginning of slavery. With it comes the concept of a class society based on the exclusive ownership of private property. This legal property concept, Marx argues, has followed the development of division of labor. In the preslave stage, exclusive ownership was meaningless since the tools were owned simply by those who used them in the family and tribal division of labor. No exploitative relationship was implied in these primitive societies, but in the slave economies the slave not only was owned himself but was required to work the land of others. Ownership of land meant, to Marx, the opportunity to use the productive labor factor and hence was the means of exploitation. As such, land becomes synonymous with wealth, and society becomes stratified on this basis. The democracy of barbarism lapses into the aristocracy of the classical world. Marx interprets the decline of the democracy of Greece and the fall of the republic in Rome as the demise of the institutions of the tribe in favor of the imperial slavocracy. The ideology of the aristocracy follows from its material relations. A Cicero who stood for the old gentile order was doomed no matter how brilliant his defense of the republic. The inevitable march of history produced a Caesar to bring it to an end.

The influence of economic factors in historical development is certainly evident in this account of ancient history. In fact, as Bernstein points out, the earlier stages of society were more closely constrained by the problem of survival, and the congruence between production and social institutions was more pronounced. But even at this stage it seems clear that Marx must depart from a monistic materialist interpretation of the social changes which took place. For instance, what influence requires that captives or newcomers to a tribe be enslaved rather than simply accepted into the egalitarian tribal division of labor? [33] It would seem that Marx has to develop an acquisitive theory of human nature, as Bober suggests,[34] which would eliminate the possibility of ultimate improvement of man in the socialist utopia; or he has to give equal weight to a continuing

predatory ideology of barbarism's hunting stage with the economics of slave production. Of course not even a slaver can
create a material surplus out of tradition alone; but the existence
of slavery presupposes that the individuals in the ruling society
must have a predisposition to exploit others. Why else would the
technology that produces a surplus imply the *legal* relationship
of property ownership? The material monistic theory of history
is self-contradictory if it has to accept the force of ideology of the
predisposition to exploit others to account for such nonmaterial
influences as the notion of exclusive control over property.[35] The
predatory ideology of exploitation can be presented as the *other*,
derived from the previous hunting material economic relations,
and the two by interaction produce the new slave system. This
might serve as a verification of Marx's theory. But Marx must
then define ideology as all received tradition and trace its material origin back to some nebulous primeval animal relation
with environment. Interpreted this way his theory is incapable
of testing the primacy of material motivations in operationally
forecasting events.[36]

Marx concedes that the growth of the surplus in classical society permits the growth of a leisure class with time for intellectual pursuits. While ideas develop through pure intellectual criticism and ratiocination and so may have a modifying force on
the course of events, nevertheless they are constrained by the
fundamental material environment of the slave economy. The
reason for the persistence of slavery, he says, is to be found
not in the great importance of economic compared to intellectual
factors in human motivation but in the essential material nature
of society.

Marx's theory advances to an account of the decline of slavery
and the rise of feudalism. This is probably the least satisfactory
transition in his work since he has to establish the technical
superiority of the small-scale manorial system over the latifundia.
Actually the transition process, insofar as it is discussed at all, is
presented by Engels who describes how the acquisitiveness of

Roman society led to wars, taxation, soil depletion, and the impoverishment of the market for farm produce.[37] The resultant decline of the exchange economy was the revival of subsistence agriculture. While Engels establishes that the barbarian invasions were of minor importance in the long run, he does so by showing that the cause of the decline is commercial and military and that production adapted to these elements of superstructure rather than the other way around. This is interesting in light of the Weber thesis suggesting that had the cultural and specifically religious superstructure been different in Rome, capitalism might have arisen on the basis of the Roman proletariat rather than developing into a feudal society. Weber suggests that the development of capitalist institutions was under way in the Roman republic only to be interrupted by the Empire with its ideology of wealth through spoils of conquest, tax farming, and bureaucratic world-empire. These institutions served to obstruct the development of a profit-maximizing (*rational*) industrial bourgeoisie from the commercial enterprises already active.[38] It follows from this that the growth of capitalism depended more on the development of Protestantism than on the completion of the intermediate stage of feudalism. While the economics of capitalism certainly is a causal factor in the rise of Protestantism, as Marx suggests, it appears equally likely that the religious ideology may have served as a causal factor. It hardly seems as if the evidence points exclusively to the primacy of either; we may, in fact, be arguing over an attempt to assign priority to chickens or eggs.

Under feudalism, argues Marx, there is no concealing the exploitative nature of the labor process.

For the reason that personal dependence forms the groundwork of society there is no necessity for labor and its products to assume a fantastic form different from their reality. They take the shape, in the transactions of society, of services in kind and payments in kind. . . . Compulsory labour is just as properly measured by time, as commodity producing labour; but every serf knows that what he expends in the service of his lord, is a definite quantity of his own personal labour-power.[39]

Marx regards any suggestion that the lord of the manor might have been productive in providing the social overhead of local defense and government as the *reductio ad absurdum* demonstration of an argument for the productivity of nonlabor factors.[40] With the rise of capitalism and the revival of production for exchange Marx argues that the proletarian is in the same historical exploited position as the medieval serf and the earlier slave. Since labor is the only productive element, the existence of profit— interest and rents, collectively surplus value—is evidence of exploitative unearned income. All this exploitation takes place while labor is personally free to sell its energies to the highest bidder. Consequently, exploitation takes the form of surplus labor value. Exploitation in the democratic state results in a class dictatorship, even though it appears to afford equal rights to all its citizens.

Further, Marx continues, just as the slave, feudal, and capitalist societies came into being by the destruction of earlier institutional forms which stood in the way of advancing technology, so socialism as a higher form of organization for production will replace capitalism. The collective mode of production within the factory (including its supervisory labor) will inevitably destroy individual ownership of the factory. The contradiction between individual ownership and social production will lead to the breakdown of the private ownership system of production and will bring about the social revolution.

II · Value

However great the faith Marx placed in his philosophy of history, its specific reference to capitalism had to be established. Not only was this a practical necessity for Marx the revolutionist, but it was also a consequence of the nature of dialectical deduction which can supply the sanction of historical necessity for events only after the fact. Marx had to show that a society which presents itself as an immense accumulation of commodities obeys the same historical laws he posited for earlier societies. Specifically he had to show: (1) how the commodity form of market exchange results in class conflict and exploitation of the labor force; (2) how the commodity system will fail to function as a result of the unfolding of its own imminent contradictions; (3) why the class conflict under capitalism, unlike those of earlier epochs, should result in the rule of the formerly exploited class rather than give rise to a new ruling class.

The market mechanism is the device used by capitalist society to allocate its commodity resources. For Marx, the analysis of the market and its process of valuing commodities was the means whereby the allocative mechanism of capitalism could be understood. In this Marx was at one with most other theorists of the capitalist economy who, in examining the market mechanism, analyzed how well it works in terms of its own goals. But for Marx the analysis of value also had to dispute the goals of capitalist society itself. The familiar phenomena of market supply and demand had to be shown to be the superficial form of a more profound entity, labor value, which would relate capitalism to a dialectical theory of the history of different modes of production.

Value, Metaphysics, and History

The key role that value plays in Marxism, then, can be best understood in the historical perspective in which Marx placed it. He says it is the means whereby the labor process and the exploitation of the toiling propertyless class represents itself under capitalism.

It is one of the chief failings of classical economy that it has never succeeded, by means of its analysis of commodities, and, in particular, of their value, in discovering that form under which value becomes exchange-value. . . . The reason for this is not solely because their attention is entirely absorbed in the analysis of the magnitude of value. It lies deeper. The value form of the product of labor is not only the most abstract, but is also the most universal form, taken by the product in bourgeois production, and thereby gives it its special historical character. If then we treat this mode of production as one eternally fixed by nature for every state of society, we necessarily overlook that which is the *differentia specifica* of the value-form. . . .[1]

If the essence of any society were to be found in the labor activity of its members in physical production, then it follows that a theory of value had to be founded on the production process of capitalism. In some ultimate sense, production for exchange which was characteristic of capitalism should reflect the physical relation of man to nature rather than the apparent characteristics of market supply and demand.

Under feudal society, Marx has it, the division of labor and the allocation of resources to various purposes was accomplished by the ruling class by a combination of force and tradition. Under capitalism, however, men meet each other as equals on the market and hence the freedom of arriving at a contract not only must subsume exploitation but must bring order into the apparent disorder of individual self-seeking bargains. "In a community of commodity producers, this qualitative difference between useful forms of labor that are carried on independently by individual producers, each on their own account, develops into a complex system, a social division of labor." [2]

It was to the key economic variable of value, then, that Marx turned to explain the division of labor which underlay the apparent anarchy of capitalist production. In this Marx reiterated the Ricardian concept of labor as the measure of relative values. The value configuration served to solve the microeconomic problem of the allocation of resources in a market economy.

But Marx went further than the labor theory of value in the Ricardian model in which, as a first approximation, labor input in an average product might be taken as proportional to all factor costs.[3] Labor, for Marx, was what Dobb calls a "unique social cost," representing the economic embodiment of the human activity of wresting a living from nature. In *capitalism* it appears as a mass of exchangeable commodities. The important feature of this theory for Marxism is that it should abstract entirely from subjective determination. Since man's mental activity is determined—at least in the final analysis—by his material relationships to his environment, it would be inadmissible to have his expression of this relation under capitalism as value to be determined by any subjective or psychological cost. Indeed Marx was trying to prove the reverse: Subjective attitudes such as peoples' willingness to buy at different prices are determined by material conditions of labor and the technology of its use.

To establish that labor is the essential universal of social evolution as Marx claimed to have done for earlier societies is not enough here. It has to be shown that commodities are actually exchanged according to the labor expended in their manufacture in capitalist society. In other words Marx has to show, at least in the long run, that the prices of goods tend to converge specifically to their labor value rather than a determinate price equilibrating many costs so that he may subsume capitalism under the laws of history which we examined in the previous chapter.

But *is* there a *unique* social cost? (Does the inverse of a social welfare function have *one* independent variable, labor?) Marx has no doubts about this; and it is here that dialectics determines economics. We have noted that dialectical materialism cannot deduce particular events from general principles; Marx's statements are discovered empirically and only receive their status as dialectically necessary after the fact.[4] The dialectical terms in which Marx surrounds his exposition of value in *Capital* might then be considered simply as the superfluous window dressing for empirical conclusions. It may safely be considered a harmless exercise in semantics. This would be so were it not for the methods of the social sciences entailing extensive selection of facts to be considered relevant by the investigator. Furthermore, the conclusions drawn on the basis of philosophical preconceptions determine the *constitutive ceteris paribus* assumptions implicit in any empirical investigation. What kind of statement qualifies as a *fact* to be considered? The conclusions are contained in the method.

The deduction of the labor theory of value involves just this sort of interdependence of Marx's philosophy and economics. Indeed his specifically economic theory of value is most vulnerable just at this point. For Marx assumed that there had to exist an essence, a *quality*, which is common to commodities in order to make them commensurable. This quality had also to be expressed in the quantitative, intensive, magnitude of value to solve the allocation of resources problem. Marx says, "first: the valid exchange of values of a given commodity expresses something contained in it, yet distinguished from it."[5] This is the key sentence in Marx's entire work, because it is the statement of the existence theorem. There *is* a single substance which inheres in commodities and governs their exchange.

Having granted this premise, all that is required is the examination of various possibilities until, by a process of elimination, the common factor is found. This, of course, turns out to be the labor time expended in the production of the commodity. But no justification is given for the existence theorem in *Capital*. The lack of any defense of the existence of a solution seems to indicate that Marx did not feel one was required. To the Hegelian rationalist, it is no more possible to conceive of the price of commodities being determined by the equilibrium of the multiplicity of historically evolved forces which determine the shape of individual subjective patterns of preferences, than it is to imagine any multiplicity of historical causes. There cannot be many universals from which value could be deducted without there also being a common ground governing them relative to each other (Spinoza). There has to be a single overriding law governing succeeding stages of the equilibrium point of the supply and demand forces. A statement of price as determined by the equilibrium of a contingent series of psychological attitudes manifesting themselves as acts of choice is not an explanation at all. There has to exist an ultimate explanation of which price is but the "phenomenal form." Marx is looking for the "crystals of . . . social substance." [6]

In our brief investigation into rationalist philosophy we saw how the assumption of a necessary connection between events without empirical justification leads to the deduction of those metaphysical entities which Berkeley labeled "occult substances." These unobservable substances become increasingly insubstantial and abstracted from reality as the rationalists become more scientifically sophisticated and consequently less able to find place for these substances in the physical world. The Hegelian category of "essence" is the ultimate outcome of this rarification and underlies Marx's belief in a social substance, value. [7]

The transcendental nature of Marx's value concept is made evident by his discarding of price as the key economic variable. Price is the obvious proximate basis on which exchange actually does take place. Marx, however, does not wish to deal with observed price phenomena. These are the accidental ratios at which goods exchange as opposed to "value" which is the ultimate determinant of price:

The price or money-form of commodities is, like their form of value generally, a form quite distinct from their palpable bodily form; it is, therefore, a purely ideal or mental form. Although invisible, the value of iron, linen, and corn has actual existence in these very articles: it is ideally made perceptible by their equality with gold, a relation that, so to say, exists only in their heads. Their owner must, therefore, lend them only his tongue, or hang a ticket on them before their prices can be communicated to the outside world. . . . Every trader knows that he is far from having turned his goods into money, when he has expressed their value in a price. . . .[8]

Value must be an objective property of the individual commodity and yet commensurable between commodities. The property cannot be a physical dimension since it is specific to the commodity and exchange value is a universal attribute of all commodities. He eliminates use values because he considers them also to be particular properties of individual things: "As use values, commodities are, above all, of different qualities, but as exchange values they are merely different quantities, and consequently do not contain an atom of use value. . . ." Utility, to Marx, is a singular property of the thing rather than a state of mind: "If we make abstraction from its use-value, we make abstraction from the material elements and shapes that make the product of a use value." [9]

Therefore, any attempt to determine value by comparing utility is not only measuring an incommensurable but attempting to reduce the social act of exchange between people into a relationship between things. This "fetishism of commodities" is the source of the misconceptions of bourgeois economists, said Marx:

A commodity is . . . a mysterious thing, simply because in it the social character of men's labour appears to them as an objective character stamped on the product of that labour . . . a definite social relation between men, that assumes in their eyes, the fantastic form of a relation between things.[10]

To Marx it is utterly inconceivable that utility can be a universal within the mind of the consumer or seller of factors of production. Like Spinoza and Hegel he assumed that there can be only one Substance of which all particulars are moments; the Substance is material: Hence utility is not a universal, subjectively comparable, valuation, but rather must inhere in and derive from matter. To Marx use value is inevitably as particular as the individual properties of the things which are commodities. Utility theorists would say it is the act of human valuation which makes utility a universal concept subject to degrees of intensity. Their disputes turn on whether the utility of the choices made by individuals can be arranged in amounts of utility or whether the consumer merely ranks his satisfaction.[11] Marx eliminates a utility theory of value by refusing to consider utility except as it can be shown to be derived from the changes in the true universal, matter, rather than by showing the inadequacy of the theory to explain events. In this he is consistent with the elimination of *individual*—as opposed to the social—consciousness by materialistic philosophy except as a practical reaction to material reality.

The process of elimination is now complete: "If then we leave out of consideration the use-value of commodities, they have only one common property left, that of being products of labor." [12]

Competition forces the ideal estimates of the ratios of exchange by potential buyers and sellers to conform to the material reality of the labor consumed in their production. It is worth repeating the point that price, the "magnitude of value," might have been determined directly by the interaction of these ideal estimates until the subjective valuations are in equilibrium. But Marx's materialism requires a rationalist explanation: The direction of causation cannot be from the ideal valuation to the objective exchange ratio. A scientific explanation must go from material to ideal. The labor value of gold, the money commodity, provides the basis for the ideal valuations. Money: "As the measure of value . . . serves to convey the values of all the manifold commodities into prices, into imaginary quantities of gold." [13]

Subjective valuation of the utility of an object has absolutely no meaning for Marx. He conceives value derived from material relationships to be logically prior to price. "The utility of a thing makes it a use value. But this utility is not a thing of air. Being limited by the physical properties of the commodity, it has no existence apart from that of the commodity." [14]

In this way Marx is led by his philosophy to search for the objective substance of value which I contend has no empirical meaning:

The exchange, or sale of commodities at their value is the rational way, the natural law of their equilibrium. It must be the point of departure for the explanation of deviations from it, not vice versa the deviations as the basis on which this law is explained.[15]

We can observe prices and we can observe the "revealed preference" of the tongue, but we do not and cannot observe value. Why not simply jettison the concept as a metaphysical philosophers' stone?

There are two Marxist replies. The first is associated with the two leading English-speaking Marxist economists, Maurice Dobb and Paul M. Sweezy. They argue, in effect, that it is possible to speak meaningfully of a theoretical variable which is itself not directly observable. Following the empiricist philosopher Braithwaite, we would agree that if certain observed events were to be inexplicable without introducing the value concept then we would be compelled to introduce it as a meaningful hypothesis. In the field of exchange the refinement of Marshallian economics shows that it is not necessary to go beyond the immediate facts of observable consumer choice to account for market phenomena. But Dobb suggests that there are events, not involved in price determination, which could be included in a more general deductive system by the introduction of the notion of value. His view is that the application of the general materialist view of exploitation by classes of owners of the means of production to capitalism requires the acceptance of the labor theory of value. Far-reaching predictions about the rise and fall of social orders then become available. Dobb is thus willing to accept the labor theory of value with all its limitations in order to arrive at this revolutionary view of history.

This may explain Dobb's *desire* for a more general theory, but it should not be construed as an argument in support of the labor theory itself. Dobb puts it as a fact that historical materialism—labor exploitation and necessarily intensifying class struggle —is a necessary characteristic of capitalism; and the theoretical explanation of this necessity requires the acceptance of the labor theory of value. This approach, however, immediately leads to the question of the logical status of the materialist conception of history. Can it really be thought of as an observed, factual account of the historical process? Hume pointed out that no causation or necessity can be observed. This is true, a fortiori, of dialectical necessity. Is the labor theory of value necessary to explain the fact of poverty and social upheaval which is observed? Not necessarily. There may be a multiplicity of causes.

Marx and Engels reverse Dobb and appear to view the work of *Capital*, especially the labor theory of value, as a verification of historical materialism. Here the argument about succeeding stages of labor exploitation by ruling classes is a general principle which may also be applied to capitalism. Now if historical materialism were actually a deductive theory, the wages system, exploitation, labor-exchange-value would all be contained in the premises of the system and could be deducted from it. If this were so then the labor theory of value and the consequent doctrine of surplus value would serve as potential falsifiers of a meaningful materialist conception of history. If the labor theory of value could be observed as false, historical materialism would also be false. If the labor theory were the best explanation of market phenomena then historical materialism would be thus far verified. Marx apparently thought that while the observation of value was indirect, it was the only worthwhile explanation of exchange and served as a meaningful and successful test of this historical theory.

In fairness it must be admitted that in Marx's time the classical labor theory in what Mill and McCulloch took to be its Ricardian form was orthodoxy among economists. We are more concerned, here, however, with the doctrine rather than its author.[16] To test this doctrine it must be shown that the carrying out of the test does not require the acceptance of the theory being tested.

Otherwise, the whole procedure is a tautology. Now we have argued that before Marx can deduce the labor value by the elimination procedure he must first assume his materialist version of the doctrine of essence. There must exist a single, essential, material determinant of the acts of exchange. This rationalist assumption of a single material cause is the same assumption Marx made in justifying the theory of history. We have seen how labor was deduced as the sole productive factor. Marx, by this philosophical preconception, would have us assume the key argument of his hypothesis in order to be able to subject it to falsification.

One must assume the primacy of materialism over ideal influences before the materialist conception of history can be tested; hence test presumes its own conclusion. Nevertheless, even though we may judge the elimination method of deducing the labor theory of value to be circular in this crucial respect, we cannot close the matter here. It still remains possible that the theory might be successfully defended on other grounds. In particular, it is possible that we might be able to show that the supply and demand which we observe in the phenomenal world might tend, in their interaction, to move long-run prices toward the physical effort expended on the product. We may evaluate this possibility by asking ourselves what are the conditions for this tendency to take place? If it develops that the conditions are restricted to special cases which do not exist generally in the real world or that it is necessary to view labor as a subjective cost rather than an expenditure of physical energy, then we shall be justified in passing harsher judgment on Marx's theory than merely stating that his demonstration was inadequate.

Let us now examine supply and demand to ascertain whether value can serve doubly as the sum of the material effort of labor and the equilibrium price which allocates resources among alternative ends in the long run. This discussion, at the rigorous level which Marx's intellectual quality demands, involves using the analytical devices of price theory. The discussion of supply is presented with the hope that the reader will wish to peruse the *Appendix on Supply* yet not requiring him to do so to follow the argument presented.

Value and the Problem of Supply

Having identified the particular physical properties of commodities with use value and having eliminated these from consideration, Marx imagined that he had eliminated the differences in the physical dimensions of labor itself. Material labor was a true objective universal:

Along with the useful qualities of the products themselves, we put out of sight both the useful character of the various kinds of labour embodied in them, and the concrete forms of that labour, there is nothing left but what is common to them all: all are reduced to one and the same sort of labour, human labour is the abstract . . . the residue . . . consists of the same unsubstantial reality in each, a mere congelation of homogeneous human labor.[17]

At this juncture in the argument Böhm-Bawerk charged that Marx had contradicted himself. Böhm-Bawerk had refused to identify utility with the physical properties of commodities so that individual consumer estimates of potential satisfactions to be obtained from commodities were the psychological determinants of price through demand for scarce goods and factors of production. His marginal utility explanation of the ratio in which goods exchange on the market was subjective in nature. Böhm-Bawerk argued that Marx's theory had not really been able to deny that use value was a universal commensurable property of commodities and at the same time assert that abstract labor was. Marx, of course, realized that the actual performance of labor involved many different types of work. "Concrete labor," as Marx called it, in its phenomenal form was not the universal "abstract labor" with only intensive magnitudes, but was heterogeneous depending on the concrete physical properties of the labor and the product. In a key paragraph Böhm-Bawerk says:

Is it possible . . . that exactly the same evidence on which Marx formulated his verdict of exclusion against the value in use holds good with regard to labor? Labor and value in use have a qualitative side and a quantitative side. As the value in use is different qualitatively as table, house or yarn, so is labor as carpentry, masonry or spinning. And just as one can compare different kinds of labor according to their quantity, so can one compare values in use of different kinds according to the amount of the value in use.[18]

Böhm-Bawerk's question is not fruitfully discussed by asking whether Marx had inadvertently contradicted himself. Marx was aware of the problem and thought he had justified the use of abstract material labor. The interesting issue is whether the reduction of concrete labor to abstract labor is successful or entails the use of subjective valuations. For Marx, any concrete labor must be shown as "counting" as some multiple of the least skilled, "simple" labor in the determination of value in which the multiplier is not a subjective valuation.

Dobb attempts to dismiss the problem too easily with the remark: "The assumption of homogeneity of units of a factor of production is common to economic method up to the present day." [19] It is true that the assumption is made, but it is done in two different contexts: *Analytically*, the subjective valuation of the disutility involved in performance by even the most diverse factors of production can be reduced to homogeneous money valuations if the factors can be shown to be substitutes for other factors in the production of a particular commodity. Even if a factor were particular to a commodity and used in unvarying proportions to its output, the commodity itself has substitutes in providing consumer satisfactions. *Statistically*, the aggregation of heterogeneous factors into groups involves the acceptance of unavoidable error since, strictly speaking, the factors would then be different in character depending on the particular commodities they produce. It should be noted, however, that the error is one of measurement in grouping certain activities as "labor" as opposed to, say "entrepreneurship." The error does not arise from the process by which people value their own efforts and the technological possibilities of substitution. The statistical assumption of the homogeneity of units of a factor, then, appears only as a useful simplification adopted on practical grounds which *approximates* the actual equalization implicit in the act of choice between alternatives.

The Marxist theoretician, Hilferding, is clear on the necessity of the reduction to common units of simple labor. He says that "only if I am able to express this whole in terms of some common unit of measurement can I regard it as qualitatively homogeneous." [20] Hilferding's own solution, however, which runs in terms of "latent skilled labor," introducing a new metaphysical entity, need not be taken seriously. Marx's own pronouncements on the subject are far from unambiguous, but I think it is fairly safe to assume that he had a reduction solely in terms of physical productivity in mind since utility considerations were excluded *ex hypothesi*.

Marx, in an often quoted paragraph, explains the reduction:

Skilled labour counts only as simple labour intensified, or rather, as multiplied simple labour, a given quantity of skilled being considered equal to a greater quantity of simple labour. Experience shows that this reduction is constantly being made. A commodity may be the product of the most skilled labour, but its value, by equating it to the product of simple unskilled labour, represents a definite quantity of the latter labour alone.

This notion is easily subject to misinterpretation:

1. While wage differences might serve as a means of measuring the productivity of labor Marx cautions in a footnote that this is a *consequence* of the market's reduction of physical productivity: "The reader must note that we are not speaking here of wages or value that the labourer gets for a given labour time, but of the value of the commodity in which that labour time is materialized." [21]

2. Böhm-Bawerk has misinterpreted Marx's reduction as an example of circular reasoning. Marx was alleged to have determined the productivity of labor after the fact from the dif-

ferent values produced by different types of concrete labor in the same period of time. But how, Böhm-Bawerk asks, is one to know the value of goods without knowing the amount of simple labor in each concrete type of labor? This information is only available to the economist or businessman after the value has been determined. Böhm-Bawerk does not appreciate that Marx does not intend to determine simple labor directly since he realizes it is a transcendental entity of which price is the phenomenal form. Simple abstract labor is not directly measurable. Price, fluctuating with shifts in the equilibrium of supply and demand, spontaneously tends toward labor value, but the individual in the economy need not, and indeed cannot, *ex ante,* determine the amount of abstract labor involved.

What are the determinants of the multipliers by which concrete labors are equilibrated to simple unskilled labor? Marx answers that it is a matter of the relative productivities of these labors, skilled to unskilled. It must be equated "to the product of simple unskilled labour" and hence "represents a definite quantity of the latter labour alone." If the productivities are to be compared, then it follows that the labors must be substitutes for one another; the comparison must be accomplished by whoever is directing production in light of his knowledge of the technical relationships of input and output, the production function.

It is sometimes alleged that Marx did not conceive of alternate combinations of factor inputs. It is true that the problem of choosing among them would then be nonexistent since there would be only one technique. But then the valuation problem would be completely insoluble since there would be no way to compare the inputs.[22]

If at any point in time, we take the production function as given, we must conceive of a circumstance in which the subjective estimates of the dissatisfactions of alternative occupations by a laborer are irrelevant to the valuation of the labors, that is, to their relative productivity. How do the subjective valuations intrude themselves into the productivity of each input? Clearly the valuation is accomplished through the decisions of the laborer on *how much* of each type of labor he wishes to expend. Only if the productivity of each concrete labor were independent of the amount of it expended in combination with other concrete labor could the subjective valuation be avoided. Such a production function, then, amounts to a denial of the law of diminishing returns which makes the rate of technical substitution of factors depend on the amounts of them employed. Marx, like Ricardo, tended to think of the law of diminishing returns in the sense of firms differently circumstanced, each of which produced under constant costs. A little reflection, however, makes it clear that the difference in circumstances themselves corresponds to the relative availability of factors (such as land) relative to others and is implicit in Ricardo's discussion of intensive as well as extensive margins of production.

The denial of diminishing returns runs into serious difficulty if we consider wageworkers instead of independent producers who may expend their budget of energy in different ways doing different types and amounts of labor. In the case of the self-employed artisan or peasant producer the dissatisfaction of an additional unit of each type of labor depends on the amount of it employed and increases to the extent that variation in work decreases. Put differently, given a "budget" of effort to be expended, more time will be expended with the same disutility if the laborer mixes his work rather than sticks to his last. This permits a solution to the problem of choice of input amounts for the individual producer; he can get the output for a given effort by altering the disutility ratio of each type of labor by changing the amounts used until the ratio of additional disutilities equals the relative productivities of these labors according to the production function. But if the relative valuation in wages of "labor power" of different labors is determined by the labor cost of reproducing and training the laborer—or indeed if it is any constant market price—then there is no reason to believe that the

technical rate of substitution implicit in the elimination of diminishing returns will coincide with the relative labor values. If they
do *not* coincide, then only *one* labor type will be used and *none*
of its substitutes; if they *do* coincide, then *any* combination of
labor inputs will be *equally* satisfactory. Both these alternatives
do violence to choice although the latter might be rescued by
reference to tradition or even accidental determinations. The
difficulties do not end here for, if for any combination of labor
activities the ratio of wages must equal the ratio of labor expended, in some manner the two must be compared by the wage
earner. This ratio—which is Marx's rate of surplus value plus
one—requires once more that a measure be made by the people
concerned of the relative disutility of labor and the compensa-
tions of work. If the same laborer has alternative occupations
then he does not simply adjust to the technology, but by choosing work makes a subjective estimate of its value, just as the consumer values the product.

When one speaks of a market-wide valuation of labor or determination of rate of surplus value, further aggregation problems enter into the picture. If there is a congruence of substitution rates of inputs with disutility in one industry or firm, there
is no reason to believe that the same equality will obtain universally. If one attempts to make an *average* valuation, it must
be assumed that production functions are identical, otherwise a
shift in demand from one occupation to another would change
the weights of the valuation as well as introduce technical weight-
ing errors. This problem would remain even if the highly spe-
cialized circumstances, explored in the Appendix, obtained in
which diminishing returns and increasing disutility of labor gave
rise to a constant ratio of labor valuations for a firm.

Labor is simply not a crystallized substance: the meaning of
labor unit depends on the demand for the product which it produces and the attitudes of the persons engaged in the laboring
as well as the technology of production. Under these circumstances it is not meaningful to make comparisons over time or

between persons except imperfectly in terms of the money measure of the payment for services rendered.

We may conclude that labor is not a purely technological
materialist fact, but that it implies subjective valuations apart
from which the term has no meaning in determining human
affairs. But anticipating Böhm-Bawerk this is just the sort of
argument Marx wished to preclude. If labor were to involve subjective disutility, then there could be no objection to positive
valuation of commodities in terms of their utility.

It is for this reason that Marx criticized Adam Smith's concept
of labor as "toil and trouble." Marx says of Smith:

he has a presentiment that labour, so far as it manifests itself in the
value of commodities, counts only as expenditure of labour power,
but he treats this expenditure as the mere sacrifice of rest, freedom,
and happiness, not at the same time the normal activity of living
beings. But then he has the modern wage-labourer in his eye. More
aptly, the anonymous predecessor of Adam Smith says . . . "one
man has employed himself a week in providing this necessary of
life . . . and he that gives him some other in exchange, cannot make
a better estimate of what is a proper equivalent than by computing
what cost him just as much labour and time.[23]

Of course Smith has the modern wage laborer in his eye. Marx
has the abstract concept of labor as the human relation to nature
in his mind, but unlike Smith nothing empirically in his "eye."

Marx's objection to the subjective formulation of labor expended is also derived from the possibility of subjective sacrifices
other than labor's toil and trouble. What was there to prevent
the economist from pointing to the sacrifices of risk-bearing and
postponement of consumption? One could not deny their disutility. The consequence of Smith's version of the theory of value
is the end of any theory of an economic surplus of the Marxian
type under a perfectly competitive system. Of course, one might
say that if it were not for the institutions of capitalism these costs
would be avoided. Whatever the truth of this suggestion, the
point is that one would then be arguing that there is a *better*

form of social organization than capitalism, rather than pointing
to exploitation of labor producing surplus value which leads to
intensifying class struggles between exploiter and exploited. The
problem becomes a normative one rather than a statement of the
inherent nature of capitalism and a link to the dialectical deduction of its inevitable demise.

Value and the Problem of Demand

Marx was well aware of the subjective nature of demand.[24]
Early in *Capital* he attempts to exclude subjective consideration
from economic calculation. He comments that utility valuations
are "historically determined. To discover the various use of things
is the work of history." [25] However, from the point of view of
economics, Marx argued that while only useful things are exchanged, utility can be shown to be irrelevant to their exchange
ratios. "However important it may be to value, that it should
have some object of utility to embody itself in, yet it is a matter
of complete indifference what particular object serves this purpose." [26] Not only is the particular object of utility irrelevant for
Marx; but utility as expressed in market demand must be shown
to be irrelevant to the determination of value. Unfortunately,
Marx's presentation is made difficult by his confusion between
supply and demand conceived of as schedules and as quantities.
A schedule of demand relates the alternative quantities demanded of a commodity which consumers would be willing to
purchase out of their income with corresponding hypothetical
prices. Similarly a schedule of supply is a functional relationship between the increasing quantities of a product which would
be produced at various prices. The intersection of these two
functions determines the equilibrium price of goods at which the
amount demanded equals the quantity supplied. Although Böhm-
Bawerk credits Marx with understanding these quantities as
elastic functions of price, it is evident that he did not always
treat them as such. For instance Marx says:

If demand and supply determine the market-price, so does the market-price and in the further analysis the market value determine demand and supply. This is obvious in the case of demand, which moves in opposition to price, rising when prices fall, and falling when prices rise. But it may also be noted in the case of supply. . . .

This confusion of a determination of prices by demand and supply, and at the same time a determination of supply and demand by prices, is worse confounded by the determination of the supply by the demand, and the demand by supply, of the market by production, and of production by the market.[27]

The confusion is understandable in 1867, but as a result Marx did not make his criticism of supply and demand determinations of price clear. It is not true that "The real difficulty in determining the meaning of supply and demand is that they seem to amount to a tautology." [28] At equilibrium, of course, the amount supplied equals the amount demanded. If Marx had been willing to accept the subjective *ex ante* schedules of attitudes as meaningful instead restricting himself to *ex post* exchanges completed, he would have understood the elastic nature of supply and demand and their mutual equilibration. He would then not have fallen into the confusion of mutual determination with the identity of amounts supplied and demanded. Marx's fundamental point is different. At equilibrium supply and demand must be identical phenomenal ways of expressing value. Marx argues that *ex ante* schedules of demand and supply and short-run prices are deviations from, but inadequate to, a determination of long-run exchange ratios. Value must be a prior materially determined ratio of exchange toward which prices gravitate and subjective attitudes adjust.

Nothing is easier than to realize the inequality of demand and supply, and the resulting deviation of market-prices from market-values. The real difficulty consists in determining what is meant by supply and demand.

Demand and supply balance one another, when their mutual proportions are such that the mass of commodities of a definite line of production can be sold at their market-value, neither above nor below it. That is the first thing we hear.

The second is this: If the commodities are sold at their market-values, then supply and demand balance.

If demand and supply balance, then they cease to have any effect, and for this very reason commodities are sold at their market-values. If two forces exert themselves equally in opposite directions, they balance one another, they have no influence at all on the outside, and any phenomena taking place at the same time must be explained by other causes than the influence of these forces. If demand and supply balance one another, they cease to explain anything, they do not affect market-values, and therefore leave us even more in the dark than before concerning the reasons for the expression of the market-value in just a certain sum of money and no other. It is evident that the essential fundamental laws of production cannot be explained by the interaction of supply and demand (quite aside from a deeper analysis of these two motive forces of social production, which would be out of place here). For these laws cannot be observed in their pure state, until the effects of supply and demand are suspended, are balanced, or, if they do, it is by mere accident, it is scientifically rated at zero, it is considered as not happening. . . .[29]

Nevertheless, demand enters into the Marxian system in determining the amount of commodity that is "socially necessary." Originally the concept of labor that is inefficient or wasteful is considered not socially necessary and consequently excluded from adding to value.[30] But Marx extends this idea of wasted labor to include goods that must be sold at less than their value.

Suppose that every piece of linen in the market contains no more labour time than is socially necessary. In spite of this all these pieces taken as a whole may have had superfluous labour-time spent on them. If the market cannot stomach the whole quantity at the normal price of 2 shillings a yard, this proves that too great a portion of total labour of the community has been expended in the form of weaving. The effect is the same as if each individual weaver had expended more labour-time upon his particular product than is socially necessary. . . . All the linen in the market counts as but one article of commerce, of which each piece is only an aliquot part. And as a matter of fact, the value also of each single yard is but the materialized form of the same definite and socially fixed quantity of homogeneous human labour.[31]

Thus Marx tried to avoid value determination by demand by lumping together all the labor expended by producers of a single product and saying that the value of the product is simply an aliquot part of the total labor. But how do we know that the socially necessary labor content determines the demand rather than demand determining the labor necessary to produce an additional unit of product?

The Ricardian thesis is that the ratio of goods exchange is determined both at the margin of demand and by labor expended on their production. To minimize the confusion of terms let us follow Marx and use the word *price* for the ratio of exchange determined at the margin where demand for an additional product equals the supply offered. We then reserve the word *value* for the labor content of a commodity. If the price of a good produced more than "socially necessary" falls below its value it would appear that the supply and demand are the obvious determinants of the ratios of exchange of goods and "socially necessary" is merely demand in disguise. We would jettison value unless it could be shown that in the long run demand is irrelevant to the determination of the ratios of exchange and that its influence is restricted to circumstances of short-run divergences of price from value.

Let us consider the possible circumstances under which it might be argued that demand is irrelevant to the determination of exchange at value.

One condition would be if there were an infinite elasticity of supply for commodities in the long run. That is, if commodities were produced at constant returns to inputs of labor (constant costs) regardless of the quantity fabricated, then as illustrated in Figure 1, the supply curve (S) would be horizontal. Demand would determine the amount produced (Q_1, Q_2, Q_3) depending on the location of the demand curve (D_1, D_2, D_3), but it would not affect the value (W) of the units produced.

This is the approach attributed to Ricardo by Marshall in his

celebrated Appendix I to his *Principles*. Marshall characteristically apologizes for Ricardo's emphasis on cost of production
to the disregard of demand by saying that

> though he was aware that commodities fall into three classes accord-
> ing as they obey the law of diminishing, of constant, or of increasing
> return; yet he thought it best to ignore this distinction in a theory
> of values applicable to all kinds of commodities. A commodity chosen
> at random was just as likely to obey one as the other of the two
> laws of diminishing and increasing return; and therefore he thought
> himself justified in assuming provisionally that they all obeyed the
> law of constant return.[32]

Ricardo, like Marshall, had maintained that the value as well as
the price of a commodity is determined at the margin. Consequently, whenever elasticity of supply is other than infinite, value

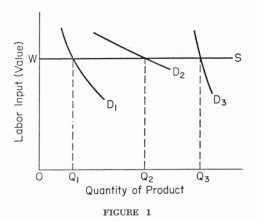

FIGURE 1

depends very much on demand. It needs further to be noted
that Marx was entirely aware of Ricardo's conclusions. Discussing the problems of supply and demand, Marx makes specific
references to them. In a chapter entitled "Market Prices and
Market Values," he says parenthetically: "See Ricardo on the
determination of the price of production by those who produce
under the least favorable conditions."[33] Marx quotes Ricardo's

discussion of this topic in full in *Theories of Surplus Value,* where he gives it careful attention.[34]

Marx's discussion shows that he is grappling with the *fact* of other than infinite elasticity of supply for many commodities. He can dismiss the temporary inelasticity as causing deviations of "actual price" from value. But the problem of increasing (or possibly decreasing) cost pervades the long-run value problem which is of greater concern to Marx. The presence in the production function of fixed factors of production—or factors of production which yield other than proportional returns to increases in their application—was noted first in Ricardo's notion of the fixed supply of land in the "original and indestructible powers of the soil." Economists have since expanded the list of limiting factors leading to diminishing returns to include scarce labor skills, uncertainty, limited entrepreneurship, restricted flows of funds, and the like, in order to explain that the long-run production function is not homogeneous in the first degree.[35] Marx sometimes appears to beg the question by arguing that the underlying costs of the schedule were different labor productivities in combination with different amounts of constant capital and land factors. Such an approach would deprive the labor theory of value of any meaning. Marshall effectively eliminated this possibility in his criticism of Jevons. He pointed out that *both* demand and supply were required as "blades of the scissors" to determine equilibrium. He argued that Jevons tried to determine equilibrium by demand only; but he might with equal logic have directed his criticism at a Marxian attempt to determine it by labor supply cost only. *Both* are required in equilibrium.[36]

The other interpretation of Marx's elimination of demand from value is clarified by recalling that the supply curve he probably had in mind is not really a hypothetical statement of the output which would be produced by the total number of firms in the industry at different prices. This Marshallian notion of supply price depends on the costs of the representative firm as it varies its output in response to the price which its products can fetch

on the market. Marx used the older form of supply in which the
scale of operations of each firm is taken as given and increases
in output are accomplished by introducing less efficient firms or
firms employing natural resources of inferior quality. This
Ricardian notion of supply was dubbed the "particular expenses
curve" by Marshall since it represents the outlay of particular
firms.[37] The particular expenses curve represents the labor
actually expended in the production by an individual firm, while
the hypothetical supply function counts labor that might be expended in a firm of average efficiency at alternative levels of
output.

In the Ricardian version, long-term price (which Ricardo
called value) is determined by the marginal firm brought into
production by demand. In general, we would then have a divergence between the mean value, $W = (a_i x_i)/n$, of labor expended
on a commodity and the price determined at the margin. This
implies that there exists an excess of surplus value in the hands
of the intramarginal firm. Further, the additional surplus value
earned by the intramarginal firms would have to be attributed
to nonlabor factors since the product of the long-run prices
charged by all firms multiplied by output would exceed the
total labor time expended in the given industry. How does Marx
attempt to escape from this predicament? I think that he gives
up the notion that long-run price and labor value are identical.

Price is determined at the margin of demand and the rising
labor cost of the particular expenses schedule. If, however, the
total labor expended on all the products in each industry were
determined by an amount considered socially necessary and if
the elasticity of demand were unity, then even though *price*
were determined at the margin, the labor expended on the total
product could remain the same. Unity in the elasticity of demand
implies that a decline in the market price would be accompanied
by an equal proportionate increase in sales so that the total
labor expended on the industry would not be greatly affected by
the labor cost of the marginal firm. The value of a unit of prod-

uct would be determined as the mean value of labor expended in these different firms. While labor expended on a unit of product might be more or less than price, depending on whether the industry operates on increasing or decreasing returns, the *sum* of the prices paid for all the produce equals the sum of the total labor which is expended on their production. This is most clearly seen in Figure 2. Here the product price, when supply is S_2 and

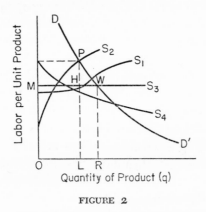

FIGURE 2

demand *DD′*, is determined at *P*; and *L* units of the product are sold. The value of a unit of the product is thus also the area under the supply curve divided by *OL*.[38] If goods were sold at their value *W* then *OR* would be sold. The area representing labor expended remains the same even though the price deviates from the mean value *W*. Marx discusses the elasticity of the particular expenses curve by referring to the concentration of firms at the upper or lower ordinates of the supply curve. If the concentration of the number of firms were in high-cost situations then the supply curve would slope upward more markedly (S_2) than it would if the firms were relatively uniform in cost function (S_1). It is even possible that there might be economies of large scale (S_4). But the degree to which unit market *prices* deviates from unit market *values* depends on the slope of the particular expenses curve. They are identical *only* where the

slope is zero, for example, curve S_3 in Figure 2. This approach
has the advantage for Marx in that he is able to permit short-run
shifts in the equilibrium price in supply due to temporary con-
strictions of the market elasticity of supply without having to
admit that the sum of prices deviates from value. By accepting
a divergence between market prices and market values, the total
labor expended on the product of any industry is made independent of the quantity demanded *at the margin.*

It should be observed that when the particular expenses curve
is S_2, I am not suggesting that the goods could be produced as
well as sold along MW, that is, S_3; they would have to be sold
at that rate, but produced the S_2 way. Were they to be produced
as well as sold at MW, the labor expended in their production
would be represented by the rectangle $OMWR$ rather than
$OMWL$. There would be an inadmissible excess of labor expended $LHWR$ when goods were sold at values rather than at
prices. It is apparent that under these circumstances value considered as a supply concept is an empty, abstract numerical
entity; it is not that goods could be produced at their value, but
only sold *as if* they were.

The confusion in terminology between demand as a schedule
and as a quantity *at the margin* makes it appear to Marx that demand, given a unit elastic demand curve, is irrelevant to value.
Price fluctuations are determined by changes in supply, but the
variations in supply price of firms do not bring about changes in
the value of the product. It is evident however that, far from
having eliminated subjective considerations, Marx has in effect
placed the burden of the labor theory of value on *demand* as the
total outlay of labor which the community is *willing* to expend
on a product. He has removed it from a supply consideration of
labor expended. Further, in order to accomplish this, he has to
assume a particular shape of this demand function with little
empirical justification.

It is true that in many passages Marx does speak of prices
fluctuating around market values without realizing that the latter

cannot be the mean value of market prices and at the same time have prices determined at the margin. But in his careful writing he gives up the idea that average price be equal to unit value and emphatically insists that it is price rather than value that is determined by production at the margin. This interpretation is supported by the following passage from *Capital*:

It is only extraordinary combinations of circumstances under which commodities produced under the least or most favorable conditions regulate the market value, which forms the center of fluctuation for the market prices, which are the same however, for the same kind of commodities. If the ordinary demand is satisfied by the supply of commodities of average value, that is to say, of a value midway between the two extremes, then those commodities, whose individual value stands below the market value, realize an extra surplus value, or surplus profit, while those, whose individual value stands above the market value cannot realize a portion of the surplus value contained in them.[39]

The balance of the translation of this key passage in the Kerr edition of Volume III of *Capital* is so misleading that it seemed worthwhile to provide my own:

It does not help at all to say that the sale of commodities produced under the worst conditions indicates that they are needed to satisfy demand. If the price were higher than the average value in the assumed situation, then demand would be greater. At a certain price a commodity occupies a certain room in the market; this room would only remain the same as prices change, if the increased price coincides with a smaller quantity of goods, and a lowered price with an increased quantity of goods. But if demand is so strong that it does not contract if price is determined by the value of goods produced under the worst conditions, then these designate the market value. This is only possible if demand is greater than usual or supply is less than usual. Finally, if the amount of goods produced is greater than the average sales at the market value, then market value will be ruled by the commodities produced under the best conditions.[40]

The Untermann translation in the Kerr edition makes it appear as if value is determined by marginal conditions. In the context of this passage as well as by a more careful translation, we may conclude that Marx means that price is determined at the margin. To be sure, if demand brings many firms into production under "the worst conditions," then the weighted arithmetic mean of labor times necessary for production will be (*bestimmen*) determined by these conditions. If supply is excessive then the central tendency of values shifts closer to the firms under lowest cost conditions and these predominate.

Marx's argument is restated with greater clarity in *Theories of Surplus Value* where the presupposition in favor of unit elasticity of demand is even more evident. There he takes Ricardo to task for saying that value is determined by the labor time in the . . . "most unfavorable circumstances; meaning . . . the most unfavorable under which the quantity of produce required renders it necessary to carry on the production."

Marx comments:

The "quantity of produce required" is not a fixed magnitude. It should read: "a definite quantity of products required within the definite limits of price." If the price rises above these limits, the quantity required falls with the demand.

The point is emphasized further where he adds:

the value of the commodity in a particular sphere of production is determined by the *total mass of social labor which the total mass of commodities of this particular sphere of social production requires,* and not by *the individual values of the separate commodities.*[41]

Marx clearly admits the subjective nature of the labor theory of value in the following passage in which he shows its ultimate determination by utility valuations of society:

If society wants to satisfy some demand and have articles produced for this purpose, it must pay for them. Since the production of commodities is accompanied by a division of labor, society buys these articles by devoting to their production a portion of its available labor-time over which it disposes. That part of society, to which the division of labor assigns the task of employing its labor in the production of the desired article, must be given an equivalent for it by other social labor incorporated in articles which *it* wants.

There is, however, no necessary, but only an accidental, connection between the volume of society's demand for a certain article and the volume represented by the production of this article in the total production, or the quantity of the social labor spent on this article, the aliquot part of the total labor-power spent by society in the production of this article. True, every individual article, or every definite quantity of any kind of commodities, contains perhaps, only the social labor required for its production, and from this point of view the market value of this entire mass of commodities of a certain kind represents only necessary labor. Nevertheless, if this commodity has been produced in excess of the temporary demand of society for it, so much of the social labor has been wasted, and in that case this mass of commodities represents a much smaller quantity of labor on the market than is actually incorporated in it. . . . The commodities must then be sold below their market-value, and a portion of them may even become unsalable. . . . But if the quantity of social labor spent in the production of a certain article corresponds to the social demand for it, so that the quantity produced is that which is the ordinary on that scale of production, and for the same demand, then the article is sold at its market value.[42]

One could not ask for a clearer statement of the subjective nature of demand for socially necessary products of labor. Far from making labor a physical expenditure of energy in a materialistic sense, this formulation eliminates supply considerations altogether from value formation and restricts it to the secondary question of price. Value is determined by how much the community is *willing* to expend in effort. While demand may shift value reflects a change in consumer tastes rather than a change in labor expended.

What Is Left of the Labor Theory of Value?

Marxist economists like Maurice Dobb realize that Marx has lost the correspondence between prices and values although they would not admit the systematic divergence that I have argued for here. The point they make is that the theory of value still permits a superior long-run analysis of the distribution of income between the essential classes of society than does the "subjective" marginalist analysis. The criticisms presented above prevent the application of value theory to the determination of wages and profits. Maurice Dobb has a valid point in stressing that the income received by an individual determines his preferences of, say, wages to leisure rather than the reverse. Prices often determine demand *schedules*. Marx himself felt that a theory of distribution had to precede logically an analysis of demand. He argued

that the "social demand" is essentially conditioned on the mutual relations of the different economic classes and their relative positions, that is to say, first on the proportion of the total surplus-value to wages, and secondly on the proportion of the various parts into which surplus value is divided (profit, interest, ground-rent, taxes, etc.). And this shows once more that absolutely nothing can be explained by the relation of supply and demand, unless the basis has first been ascertained, on which this relation rests.[43]

While it is certainly true that modern economists have been unduly content to manipulate the patterns of preferences of individuals without paying sufficient attention to what determines the preference map, it is not true that their reasoning has been made circular because changes in prices change income of some individuals which, in turn, has a reflection on the choices they make.

It would seem to me that this view confuses the feedback of income effects on demand schedules with the effect of historically accumulated *stocks of assets* and historic social conditioning of the underlying patterns of preferences which are the exogenous parameters of price theory. The income effect can be absorbed into conventional price theory as Hicks shows: As an individual's income rises he may choose to allocate his income differently between commodities or between income and leisure.[44] There is no reason why this cannot be accounted for in recording his pattern of preferences.

But the second greater question is whether the whole *preference map* is a creature of prices of commodities such as labor.

Insofar as the map is the sum of all the attitudes toward exchangeable commodities, it is affected by changes in incomes, but it is also affected by institutional conditioning, accumulation of assets, and the like. As such it is the product of historical development and while it is crucial in determining subjective attitudes it is not properly the subject of analytical deduction in price or value theory. There is undoubtedly a "feedback" of factor prices on asset accumulation, but in general not only is the preference pattern not deduced from marginalist price theory but it is not deduced by Marxian value theory either.

APPENDIX ON SUPPLY

It is most reasonable that Marx intended to say that the different qualities of concrete labor are made commensurable in the market by comparing their physical productivities in activities where they are substitutes. The abstract labor value of a commodity is determined by a general equilibrium analysis in which the production function relates different types of labor which could be employed.

I think it will be evident from the following analysis that, in all but the most restrictive of circumstances, equilibrium conditions for the valuation of heterogeneous labor inputs require that subjective estimations must be made. These can be shown to involve estimates of the disutility of effort on the part of labor or the estimation of the utility of commodities expressed as a demand schedule or both. The restrictive case implicit in Marx's system is the production of commodities by various *self-employed* types of labor which are substitutes for one another producing various goods in *identical, linear production functions.* Let us first examine this case and then extend our analysis to show that if any of these assumptions are relaxed, subjective considerations must be introduced.

In carrying out this analysis we will represent our production function which has as its independent variables the types of concrete labor $x_o, \ldots, x_i, x_j, \ldots, x_n$, rather than the classifications Marx sometimes used of time of work, intensity, and skill to which particular labors must be reduced since these are themselves *general* classifications.[45]

First assume an exchange society of self-employed laborers and let x_n be the duration of simple labor and x_j be the duration of their concrete labors. These are alternative ways in which the individual may work to manufacture his product. Then the physical product P produced by these labors in which compound labor "counts as simple labor multiplied" can be expressed:

$$P = K(x_o + a_1x_1 + \ldots + a_jx_j + \ldots + a_nx_n + C). \quad (2.01)$$

Here K represents a coefficient relating labor time to output, and a_1, a_j, and a_n are the technical multipliers by which more productive labor times must be multiplied. C is the amount of "constant capital" in machinery and semifinished goods.

The value of the product, W, is the labor expended, or

$$W = \frac{P}{K}. \quad (2.02)$$

As long as the coefficients, $a_1, \ldots, a_i, \ldots, a_n$ are constant, and hence independent of x_i, their times of labor, there are an infinite number of combinations of different types and durations of labor possible to produce a given value.

The absence of a unique solution from the production function alone giving the amount of each factor employed prevents Marx's formulation from being a complete general equilibrium. The complete solution would require the equalization of the ratio of the marginal disutility of each concrete labor with the marginal value produced by it. That is, if disutility of labor is measured by $B = L \ (x_o, x_1, \ldots, x_i \ x_j, \ldots, x_n)$, then

$$\frac{\partial W/\partial x_i}{\partial W/\partial x_j} = \frac{\partial L/\partial x_i}{\partial L/\partial x_j}. \quad (2.03)$$

But this introduction of subjective valuations which a producer might give to different types of concrete labor could be dismissed by Marx as interesting but irrelevant to his main line of inquiry. As long as there is a constant rate of technical substitution between labor factors it will make no difference in the final value whether more or less labor of a skilled type is willing to work in a particular industry. That is, if $\partial W/\partial x_i = Ka_i$ and $\partial W/\partial x_j = Ka_j$ in which x_i and x_j may be substituted for one another at a constant rate regardless of estimates of disutility since (2.03) becomes

$$\frac{a_i}{a_j} = \frac{dx_j}{dx_i}. \tag{2.04}$$

While the rate at which x_i and x_j may be substituted for one another does not vary with changes in the subjective estimates of the disutility of labor, the amount of each of the factors used and the amount of the commodity produced might be so affected. Nevertheless it is the rate of substitution which determines their relative valuation and which remains constant.[46] (The elasticity of substitution is infinite.) This can be seen graphically in Figure 3.

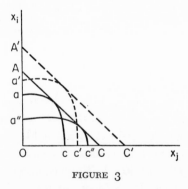

FIGURE 3

AC and $A'C'$ represent linear isoquants of the contours of the function P in the x_ix_j plane which represent all combinations of these two factors that produce equal physical output. It is the

linear nature of the production function P that makes the contours also parallel straight lines.[47] We represent the willingness
to work at alternative occupations i and j by the function B
represented by contours ac and $a'c'$. They are drawn concave
to the origin to show the increasing disutility of restricting the
individual to one type of work. More hours will be spent at
varied types of labor, x_i and x_j, with the same dissatisfaction than
if one must stick strictly to one's last. A self-employed laborer
would maximize his product subject to the constraint of the willingness to work—or the supply of labor—by engaging in occupations i and j indicated by the point of tangency of the two curves,
for example, AC and ac. If his willingness to work simply increased proportionately for both types of labor to $a'c'$ his point
of maximization would also shift. But the *rate* at which the two
types of labor count in production would not change since that
is determined by the *slope* of the isoquant. Even if changes occur
in attitudes toward different types of labor to $a''c''$—or, what
amounts to the same thing if we consider another industry with
the same production function—different amounts of concrete
labors might be employed but the slope of both the isoquant and
the disutility curve would not have changed at the point of
tangency. Under these conditions concrete labor can be considered as simple labor multiplied by a technologically determined constant.[48]

Now, let us drop the assumption that the production function
is linear. If the labor factors can be substituted in variable proportions the crucial assumption of the independence of the a and
x elements of equation (2.01) does not hold. In reality the productivity of the various labor factors depends very much on the
quantity of the factor employed. We must express the production
relationship of output, P, to labor inputs in the more general
functional form

$$P = P(x_o, \ldots, x_i, x_j, \ldots, x_n).$$

Here the rate of technical substitution of the labor factors depends on the quantity of each factor employed. As a result no reduction from concrete to simple labor is possible without also determining the amount of each type of labor employed. We shall see that such a general equilibrium analysis cannot ignore the subjective valuations of the laborers themselves and does not confine itself to technological relations of the production function. As before let $B = L (x_0, \ldots, x_i, x_j, \ldots, x_n)$ represent the socially necessary labor that the producer is willing to expend on the product. As such it is a labor budget constraint on the representative firm and hence on the industry.

In Figure 4, for each amount of labor, B, represented by *abc*

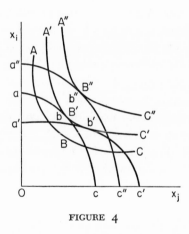

FIGURE 4

the firm will attempt to maximize its output by reaching the highest isoquant, ABC, or $A'B'C'$, and the like, at their point of tangency. We have drawn the isoquants convex to the origin to show that the new production function follows the law of diminishing returns so that fewer total hours must be spent in producing a given amount of product by moderate combinations of both labor i and j rather than using mostly one and little of the other. The rate of substitution of labor i for j is represented by the slope of the isoquant at the point of tangency with the labor budget function.

At this point where their slopes are equal we may equate the ratio of the marginal disutilities of the labor with their rate of substitution.[49] Since the slope is constantly changing as a function of x_i and x_j, the relative valuation of these labors depends on how much of them is used. This in turn depends on the shape of the B function of the disutility of labor. If this shifts from *abc* to *a'b'c'* then their valuation changes with the subjective change. Consequently the labor cost is as much a measure of subjective toil and trouble as is technological expenditure of energy in the productive process. For example, even a linear expansion path traced out on the isoquants by increasing the amounts of labor in general would be $x_i = bx_j + k$. If the intercept of the expansion path were not the origin, the ratio of labors employed, $x_i/x_j = b + k/x_j$ declines as the amount of labor x_j expended increases. Only in the special case when *both* the P and B functions were homogeneous, that is, constructed with radial symmetry around the origin, could one argue that an increase in labor (to *a"b"c"*) allocated would not change the relative valuations of concrete labor. That is to say the expansion path traced out on the isoquants by increasing amounts of labor would be a straight line through the origin, $xi = bx_j$. The marginal rates of substitution along this path would then be unchanged.

Whatever grounds there might be for arguing for an homogeneous production function, there is little justification for arguing that attitudes toward work as represented by the slopes of the corresponding points of the labor budget function remain invariant as the quantity of work increases. Changing the ratio in which value produced by concrete labors may be related at different outputs introduces the question of the intertemporal continuity of values. In the case of a nonhomogeneous expansion path a shift in demand for the quantity in question will alter its value by changing the valuation of the particular concrete labors. A fortiori changes in the attitudes toward concrete labor will change the value of the commodity. Marx solved the problem of intertemporal comparisons of labor introduced by changing technology by defining value as the labor necessary to reproduce a commodity. In the case of improved productivity, products made by obsolete methods would simply lose value and some past labor would be wasted.[50] But if the definition of abstract, simple labor, requires that account be taken of changing labor attitudes, there may be gains as well as losses of value which are the creature of the mind rather than of technology. Such changes are not only unpredictable, but they need not be consistent over time. It emerges that labor value is subject to all the objections to time comparisons of utility.

We have so far examined the problem of intertemporal comparisons of value from the point of view of a single or typical producer. Further intertemporal difficulties in the reduction to simple abstract labor arise when we attempt to aggregate the reduction ratios of the concrete labors given along the expansion path of a single producer for the many producers in various industries.[51] These labors of different industries must be commensurable in the aggregate since Marx wishes to compare the objective labor content of different products.

It is necessary that a consistent method be found whereby the ratios at which one producer evaluates his concrete labors can be averaged with the ratios of others producing different products but using at least some of the same concrete labor. There are two difficulties which arise with this procedure which, following Allen, we might identify as the problem of aggregation and the index number problem of assigning weights to the different industries. In this analysis we will assume that the objections previously raised to a linear reduction of two types of labor have been overcome either by a linear production function or by homogeneity of both the labor budget function and the production function. We will also identify as an industry firms with different reduction ratios.

The problem of aggregation involves the summation of individual reductions of the labors for one industry over n industries. That is, for the rth industry we may write

$$x_{ir} = a_r x_{jr}. \tag{2.05}$$

We wish to aggregate this micro relationship to the macro relation

$$x_i = a x_j$$

where

$$x_i = \sum_r x_{ir}, \tag{2.06}$$

and a is the average of the reduction coefficients $a = \bar{a} = 1/n \sum_r a_r$. But if a_r is different for each industry, equation (2.06) will only hold if $x_j = 1/\bar{a} \sum_r a_r x_{jr}$. In other words x_j is *weighted* by the marginal rate of substitution, a_r, peculiar to each industry rather than $x_j = \sum_r x_{jr}$, the simple sum of the hours at which x_j labor is employed. Had we written down the aggregate relationship (2.06) which is required in Marx's theory we would find that the value of the reduction coefficient $a = x_i/x_j$ is not the average of the reduction coefficients of the various industries. All this boils down to saying that the aggregate of (2.05) is $x_i = \sum_r a_r x_{jr}$ which is not equal to $a \sum_r x_{jr}$. They are only equal in the very special case when the reduction ratios, a_r, are the same for all industries and hence equal to the average reduction ratios. The reduction ratio derived from the aggregate relationship will be found to vary if the amount of concrete labors x_i and x_j used change even by the amounts required by their reduction ratios.[52]

What is really involved here is that the factors of production are really only defined for a particular product since they are not equally good substitutes in others and the errors of aggregation noted above are always present when we sum across commodities.[53]

An additional difficulty involved in making intertemporal comparisons of labor involves the change in the weights attached to the various reduction ratios in computing their average value. This is the traditional index number problem of intertemporal comparisons of averages. While approximate solutions are acceptable for statistical purposes, this is inadequate for an analytical model.

How do we know that the labor at one time is the same as the labor at another if the demand pattern has varied? Clearly there are not any valid intertemporal comparisons that can be made. Labor looks less and less like a crystallized social substance.

The subjective nature of Marx's theory of value becomes evident even on the assumption of constant technical coefficients when we pass from a consideration of independent producers using their own labor to a wage economy. Let us continue to use Marx's formulation implying constant coefficients of production and a single industry. It is then possible to speak of the profit maximizing equilibrium of the firm as if it represented all the firms of the economy.

Let v_i equal the wages paid to the ith concrete labor and $\sigma_i = (a_i x_i)/v_i$, the ratio between the labor time expended on this labor and the portion of that time remitted as wages. Marx's rate of surplus value, surplus value divided by variable (wage) capital, is the ratio $(a_i x_i - v_i)/v_i$. The rate of surplus value can be easily shown to differ from σ_i by one.

The equilibrium of the firm can be represented as the maximization of production subject to the budget constraint. This latter is the sum of all the wage payments plus the cost of replacement of value produced in time past, that is, constant capital k.

If for geometrical purposes we consider only two labor factors i and j, then we draw linear isoquants (AB, $A'B'$, $A''B''$, ...) and the linear budget constraint (ab). We represent another set of linear isoquants by ($\alpha\beta$, $\alpha'\beta'$, ...). It is intuitively obvious from the Figure 5 that if both the isoquants and the budget constraint are linear there are two ways in which the highest isoquant subject to the budget constraint can be reached. If the isoquants are not parallel to the budget constraint, such as the set $\alpha\beta$, $\alpha'\beta'$, then the maximum output can be obtained by using one factor of production exclusively. In this case only x_i would be used and would correspond to a point α''. If both factors are to be used then the isoquants AB, $A'B'$ must be parallel to ab and consequently equilibrium is reached where

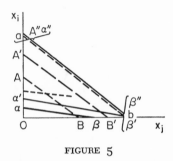

FIGURE 5

they coincide. The firm may maximize its output anywhere along ab and $A''B''$. Since the linear isoquant is a line not only of equal product but of equal value and since the budget line represents points of equal wage bill, it follows that the ratio of value produced to labor must be the same for all points on the lines. In other words σ_i and consequently the rate of surplus value, must be the same for all types of labor employed in this industry.[54]

How is this to be achieved? Can the wage level be determined only by the labor time necessary to reproduce the laborer? If so, then the employer would demand only the one type of labor that would yield the highest return since there are no diminishing returns if we are given a linear production function. The only possibility is that the slope of the labor budget line reflecting the ratio of wages paid i and j changes as more of the labor is used until it is equal to the value produced by each of these labors. That is, wages are adjusted to be proportional to the value of the marginal product of each of the types of labor so that the rate of surplus value is the same for each of them. On Marx's assumptions the demand side of this equilibrium may be technological, that is, the marginal product with respect to labor skill-and-intensity, but the supply side must reflect the balancing of the worker's estimate of his labor effort against the wage compensation he receives. We can see this by writing the equivalent in simple labor time (x_n) for each of the concrete labors

$$x_1 \ldots x_i \ldots x_n:$$
$$x_{n1} = a_1 x_1,$$
$$\vdots$$
$$x_{ni} = a_i x_i,$$
$$\vdots$$
$$x_{nn} = x_n.$$

Ignoring the aggregation error we sum the labor time. The value of the product is the sum of the simple labor equivalents

$$W = \sum_{i=1}^{n} x_{ni}$$

equals the average skill-and-intensity

$$a = \bar{a} = \frac{1}{n} \sum_{i=1}^{n} a_i$$

times the sum of the concrete labor times

$$x' = \sum_{i=1}^{n} x_i,$$

that is, $W = ax'$. Then the demand for another unit of labor skill-and-intensity is given as the constant increase in value provided by such an increment.[55] But if a situation is to be avoided in which, all other things being the same, different rates of return accrue to capitalists using different labors (as well as different amounts of effort and skill being expended by the workers for the same compensation), the worker must compare his wage with some subjective estimate of skill-and-intensity and embody it in a supply curve for labor power. The market clears at a single σ as illustrated in Figure 6. The linear nature of the de-

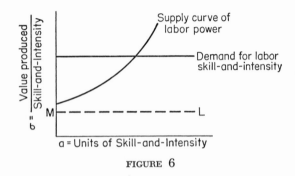

FIGURE 6

rived demand for skill-and-intensity determines the necessary rate of surplus value for equilibrium. But unlike the case of the self-employed laborer with linear production functions, the separation of labor from the entrepreneur who received the return of the labor expended requires that the worker must adjust his supply of the skill-and-intensity to his own reward for any equilibrium to be achieved. If the supply curve for labor were simply independent of σ as in ML there might be either a zero or infinite demand for labor power depending on whether it lies above or below the demand for skill-and-intensity. Now differences needed for a schedule relating the wage rate to skill cannot simply be stated as the cost of rearing and training laborers. This begs the question since clearly the decision to enter an occupation itself depends on the balance of the rewards and efforts required.[56]

The supply price of labor, then, is seen as more than the reproduction costs of different types of labor, but reflects the worker's subjective estimate of the disutility of work. Sweezy treats the equalization of surplus value as the result of the elimination of differential geographical wage patterns. He says:

Marx almost always works with the simplifying assumption that the rate of surplus value is the same in all branches of industry. . . . This assumption implies . . . a homogeneous, transferable labor force. . . . Workers do move out of low wage areas.[57]

But what is really involved is the marginal equalization of income against effort. No matter how Marxists try to avoid this conclusion the labor of human beings cannot be generally treated as being at once a technological datum and also a force governing the laborers' conduct without at some point in the argument permitting them to evaluate labor and its product as it affects their consciousness. Consciousness expressed as act of choice and the price measures of these mental attitudes stubbornly refuse to disappear in the face of materialist monism.

In the course of discussing the problem of the formation of a uniform average rate of profit for all capitals, Marx admits this equalization process:

If capitals employing unequal amounts of living labor are to produce unequal amounts of surplus value, it must be assumed, at least to a degree, that the intensity of exploitation, or the rate of surplus value, are the same, or that any existing differences in them are balanced by real or imaginary (conventional) elements of compensation. This would presuppose a competition among the laborers and an equilibration by means of their continual emigration from one sphere of production to another.[58]

In Volume III of *Capital* Marx defines the prices of production at which goods are actually sold as different from their values. Prices adjust so that the rate of profit be equalized between firms. Since the profit rate is calculated on total capital advanced (variable and constant), while it is produced as a multiple of wage-labor employed (rate of surplus value), it is necessary that firms enter industries with low constant capital to total capital ratios lowering selling price from values to prices of production. Those firms which remain in industries with a high constant capital ("organic") composition will sell at prices of production which exceed values. In this way a redistribution of surplus value is obtained. In order for this not to invalidate the conclusions drawn from value theory the sum of profits must equal the sum of surplus value, *ex ante* the laborers must produce as much surplus value as appears *ex post* after the redistribution by intra-capitalist competition. Since the capitalist does not calculate surplus value, but rather the *ex post* phenomenal category of profit, the worker must be relied upon to make subjective comparisons between total labor and wage compensation. The form of comparison which Marx accepts would be to leave the rate of exploitation unchanged by the redivision of surplus value.

III · The Wage Bargain

Laborer's Price: The Great Contradiction

The critical value for Marxian political economy is that of labor. The application of the theory of value to the hire of free proletarians in the open market determines whether exploitation of the propertyless continues under democratic governments dedicated to equality of political franchise. If the equality of the freely competitive market were to parallel political equality, then competition would rule out any systematic cheating of the laborers by their employers. Workers have to be paid the value of the commodity they sell. For Marx payments to factors of production had to be accounted for in a manner compatible with a theory which imputed all value produced to labor and at the same time managed to reward nonlabor factors, that is, capitalists, landlords, money-lenders, and the like.

Thus Marx found himself embroiled in a contradiction which was the heritage of David Ricardo's criticism of Adam Smith. Marx took as a tenet of classical thought that labor was the determinant of the value of all commodities. As such it had to be a common quality of all commodities and yet not a commodity itself. If the standard of value were a commodity, then one would demand what determined the value of the standard itself and the economist would be involved in an infinite regress. Adam Smith was ambiguous on this point. On some occasions he would refer to the "labor commanded," that is, the reciprocal of the wage rate, as the determinant of value, and at others he would speak of labor expended. Ricardo pointed out that these were not identical. If "labor commanded" were the standard, then Smith must have been talking of a commodity as the standard. The infinite regress then turned on the value of the labor commanded. What determined the wage rate?

At the same time the Ricardian critique itself failed to adequately answer how labor expended could be the determinant of value and still account for profit. If labor were paid the value of its product, labor expended and wages would be identical and there would be nothing left in the national product for payments to other factors. The compensation of the laborer then had to be the commodity equivalent of the labor commanded by his wages, and yet it seemed that it could not be so.

Perhaps it was too much to ask of Ricardo, but it was already apparent from Marx's vantage point, almost a century after the publication of the *Wealth of Nations*, that Smith's ambiguous use of the term *labor* derived from the small-scale artisan capitalists—the raw materials for his analysis. Smith's great advance in economic theory lay in pointing to the three factors of production to which the value of the product might be imputed. Given his environment it was only natural that he would identify them with the labor, the toil and trouble of the working master.[1] The incomplete development of the wage system made it impossible for Smith to see that the commodity equivalent of a craftsman's product was not at the same time the labor he commanded in return for his efforts as a wage opportunity cost and also the equivalent of the labor he expended. The nub of Smith's argument, reinterpreted, is that labor is a generic term which is the equivalent of all subjective sacrifice. If so then the contradiction vanishes because payments to all factors must add up to the value of the product. But this makes the specifically labor theory of value meaningless since it amounts to saying that each factor must receive the equivalent of its subjective sacrifice—we would add at the margin—which in turn goes into making up the cost price of the individual commodity. The words *labor value* here merely mean to add the factor costs, and not that there exists a single essence of value which is to be discovered in labor.

In a critical commentary of J. B. Say's subjectivist interpretation of Smith's labor theory of value, Marx comes perilously close to discovering the superfluousness of the value concept as applied to labor. He thought that Say had reduced himself to an absurdity because this interpretation eliminated value as a meaningful concept. In Marx's words:

It is naturally still more convenient to understand by value nothing at all. Then one can without difficulty subsume everything under this category. Thus, e.g., J. B. Say: What is *"valeur"*? Answer: *"La Valeur d' une chose exprimée en monnaie."* And why has *"le travail de la terre . . . une valeur? Parce qu' on y met un* prix." Therefore value is what a thing is worth, and the land has its "value" because its value is "expressed in money." This is, anyhow, a very simple way of explaining the why and wherefore of things.[2]

Marx failed to see that Say does not lead us in the direction of a tautological expression of value in terms of what a thing is worth. Rather the price of a good is determined by an action rather than as intrinsic essence. It is valued by the act of estimating the subjective worth it would have as a substitute for commodities in general measured in money terms. It does not have an intrinsic value since "on y *met* un prix." Say is only a step away from a marginal productivity theory of income distribution. Supply of factors, like the supply of other commodities, is the disutility expressed in the price which *"on y met."*

It is true, as Marx showed, that labor cannot be said to have a measure in labor value without self-contradiction. The standard of measure must be different from the entity measured. It can however have a *price* which measures the amount of other commodities one would exchange for an additional unit of labor. Actually Marx could have absorbed the notion of a labor price into his economics but, of course, not into his philosophy of history. Early in the first volume of *Capital* Marx had to face the fact that there were commodities which were patently not the products of labor and yet fetched a price in the market. Marx's admission of this category is halfhearted and is concealed by an attempt at bourgeois morality, but the category is nonetheless there:

> Objects that in themselves are no commodities, such as conscience, honour, etc., are capable of being offered for sale by their holders, and of thus acquiring, through their price, the form of commodities. Hence an object may have a price without having a value. The price in that case is imaginary like certain quantities in mathematics. On the other hand, the imaginary price-form may sometimes conceal either a direct or indirect real value relation; for instance, the price of uncultivated land, which is without value, because no human labour has been incorporated in it.[3]

These "imaginary" commodities break down into two types: the first, representing goods which may be manufactured but are not reproducible such as works of art, "morality," and the like. The price here is the result of the inelastic supply in the face of consumer demand and is independent of the labor input. The second type is a claim on future value, such as the capitalized value of land or that of a debt instrument (later to be called "fictitious capital" in Volume III). In these cases price is determined by the intersection of reservation supply price and demand. In the first the relationship is direct; in the second it involves the mediation of a capitalizing rate of interest which in turn is regulated by the supply and demand of what Marx calls "money capital," that is, loanable funds.[4]

In the preceding chapter I argued that the search for value is the search for an occult substance which is superfluous for the determination of prices. It is now evident that it would have been possible for Marx to speak of labor having a *price* determined by supply and demand. The wage bargain considered as a contract for forward delivery of human toil and trouble can have a price just as a contract for "conscience and honor" or a capitalized claim on future surplus value can. It is curious that in his less guarded writing, in Volume II of *Capital*, Marx, feeling that the concept of surplus value is firmly established, refers to the price of labor to be performed as equivalent to the value of labor power. Apparently he is unaware that this makes the latter concept of value unnecessary. He says:

We know that the value, or price, of labor-power is paid to its owner, who offers it for sale as a commodity, in the form of wages, that is to say it is the price of a sum of labor containing surplus value. For instance, if the daily value of labor-power is equal to the product of five hours' labor value at three shillings, this sum figures in the contract between the buyer and seller of labor-power as the price, or wages for, say, ten hours of labor time.[5]

This account is clearly close to the actual bargaining process in which the demand for labor involves the marginal product that can be earned from its employment. Derived demand determines the wage bargain as much as the supply price. In other words the wage rate is determined by the supply and demand of the labor performed as price, not as value.[6]

Ricardo's rigorous review of Smith's labor theory directed Marx toward a resolution of the conflict between the labor expended and labor commanded views of wages and of value. Marx, the materialist, might have been willing to accept a demand theory of price for exceptional articles with low elasticities of supply, but for the key commodity of the capitalist system of production nothing but a material entity would do. The wage bargain cannot be a mere contract to endure the dissatisfaction of work. "In order to be sold as a commodity in the market, labour must at all events exist before it is sold. But could the labourer give it an independent objective existence, he could sell a commodity and not labour." [7]

The only possibility that remains to escape the contradiction is to replace labor as a commodity with a new commodity— labor power. "By labour-power or capacity for labour is to be understood the aggregate of those mental and physical capabilities existing in a human being, which he exercises whenever he produces a use value of any description." [8] It is the material flesh and sinews of the laborer which is sold, albeit for a specified period of time. Demand and supply can explain nothing except the ideas of the individuals as they interact, and these are useful for explaining only temporary changes in wages. Repeating the same argument that was discussed earlier in connection with values in general, Marx says of labor:

If demand and supply balance, the oscillation of prices ceases. . . . But then demand and supply also cease to explain anything. The price of labour, at the moment when demand and supply are in equilibrium, is its natural price, determined independently of the relation of demand and supply.[9]

The question immediately arises whether Marx actually succeeds in escaping from the contradiction to which the labor theory leads in which

our friend, Moneybags . . . must buy his commodities at their value, must sell them at their value, and yet at the end of the process must withdraw more value from circulation than he threw into it at starting. His development into a full-grown capitalist must take place, both within the sphere of circulation and without it.[10]

Applying the labor theory of value to labor power Marx concludes that the value of labor power is the socially necessary labor time necessary for its reproduction, that is, the labor necessary to produce the means of subsistence of the laborers. Now, since labor alone produces value, payments to all other factors represent unearned income. Therefore, the income of the capitalist and his subsequent payments to landlord and *rentier* constitute surplus value. The surplus value is the value expression of the exploitation of the propertyless class of productive workers by the parasitic owners of the means of production. By being forced by the market to put the excess of his labor time over that required to manufacture his subsistence at the disposal of the capitalist, the proletarian finds himself in the same essential class position relative to the capitalist as the earlier exploited classes of slave and serf did to their masters.

We are now entitled to ask what advance in our knowledge has been made by the introduction of the theoretical variable, *labor power,* as opposed to the phenomenal category of price of labor. Price theory accounts for wages and profits even more precisely than value. The traditional Marxian answer is that now capitalism is integrated into the dialectical deduction of history. Marxists are now able to argue that exploitation is an inevitable concomitant of capitalism, that is, the wage system. The production of surplus value implies exploitation and does not depend on the subjective attitudes of good or bad will toward labor or transitory political relationships. It is ordained by the objective exploitative class relations. Material exploitative relations, which Marx thought underlay his theory of value, determine the ideological "superstructure" so that the political class attitudes and preference patterns are derivative of class exploitation.

The doctrine of exploitation turns on Marx's philosophical conviction that value is an entity, a "social substance," rather than an equilibrium of functional relations. This idea has been expressed by saying that Marx was searching for an absolute value of commodities, rather than attempting to explain relative values in exchange. He remarks that the absolute value only becomes observable, "when placed in value or exchange relation with another commodity," yet he heaps scorn on

the modern hawkers of Free Trade who must get rid of their article at any price . . . [who] lay most stress on the quantitative aspect of the relative form of value. For them there consequently exists neither value, nor magnitude of value, anywhere except in its expression, by means of the exchange relation of commodities, that is, in the daily list of prices current.[11]

In pursuing this conviction, Marx's concept of productivity becomes identical with the expenditure of labor. The production of surplus value is the *produit net* of capitalism, rather than the production of goods and services as objects of utility. Since *ex hypothesi* it is labor only which produces value and since value like Cartesian extension cannot normally be created or destroyed, the difference between wages and value must be exploitative income to the capitalist.

Marx does not deny that capitalists (and other factors such as land) are necessary for *physical* production, under capitalist social conditions. In fact, anticipating Schumpeter,[12] he argues that they may add to the physical product by innovations and competitive reorganization of industry:

Capital now sets the labourer to work, not with a manual tool, but with a machine which itself handles the tools. Although, therefore, it is clear at the first glance that, by incorporating both stupendous physical forces, and the natural sciences, with the process of production, Modern Industry raises the productiveness of labour to an extraordinary degree, it is by no means equally clear, that this increased productive force is not, on the other hand, purchased by an increased expenditure of labour.[13]

But the physical contributions of the nonlabor factors are excluded from value calculation since there can be but one *social* cost, labor, and hence one social net product, surplus value. Marx argues that "the productive forces resulting from co-operation and division of labour cost capital nothing" because he has excluded in advance any category of cost to cover the activity of the capitalist. Productivity is the physical expenditure of human energy by wage labor for the benefit of the ruling class. As such it is distinguished from physical productivity on one hand and the endurance of subjective disutility on the other.

If value is taken as the homogeneous expenditure of human energy, the doctrine of exploitation reduces to a tautological adding up problem. As Böhm-Bawerk pointed out: By definition the sum of the labor input must equal the sum of labor expended on each product. Since the worker does not receive all the physical products in which that output is involved, Marx concludes that he is exploited. But excluding the philosophical preconception it might be equally argued that commodities embody the contributions of other factors as well. A little reflection convinces us that in the Marxian system *any* factor may be said to be exploited since the total effort of each factor does not entitle it to the whole of national income.

We conclude that the epithet of exploitation of labor in a competitive economy has no real relation to the economics of production at all; it is a philosophical preconception. Hegel had argued that the essential nature of man was practical labor. It was labor which connected him to the other world of things.[14] Marx really says as much:

In considering the labour-process, we began . . . by treating it in the abstract, apart from its historical forms, as a process between man and nature. . . . We there stated, if we examine the whole labour-process, from the point of view of its result, it is plain that both the instruments and the subject of labour are means of production, and that the labour itself is productive. . . .

Indeed material labor turns out not to always be physical for:

In order to do labour productively, it is no longer necessary for you to do manual work yourself; enough, if you are an organ of the collective labour and perform one of its subordinate functions. The first definition given above of productive labour, a definition deduced from the very nature of the production of material objects, still remains correct. . . .

In the end Marx concludes, "That labourer alone is productive, who produces a surplus-value for the capitalist, and this works for the self-expansion of capital."[15] But under a *capitalist* collective the capitalist is as necessary as a planning body is under socialism. Marx is entitled to *prefer* socialism, but that has nothing at all to do with labor's productivity and exploitation.

What Does Subsistence Mean?

If we are unwilling to accept exploitation on the grounds of the consonance ascribed to it with the dialectical materialist conception of productive labor, then we must examine the empirical content of labor power as a scientific category. In what respect does the use of this term give us economic information that is not available by a supply and demand interpretation of the price of labor? Marx had imagined that by introducing the notion of labor power he had escaped from a subjective determination of the wage bargain as a price. He had reduced it to an objective quantity subsistence, which did not depend on the ephemeral ideas of the individuals in capitalist society but which determined these ideas. He says:

In the expression "value of labour," the idea of value is not only completely obliterated but actually reversed. It is an expression as imaginary as the value of the earth. These imaginary expressions arise, however, from the relations of production themselves. They are categories for the phenomenal forms of essential relations. That in their appearance things often represent themselves in inverted form is pretty well known in every science except political economy.[16]

There are two possible interpretations of the subsistence theory of labor power. One corresponds to a meaningful and hence contingent interpretation; the other is an attempt to state the proposition that the level of wages is at subsistence as logically necessary by definition.

If subsistence wage is to be meaningful, there must be some way of defining subsistence so that the theory may be put to a test. Taken as an empirically meaningful statement *subsistence* might mean a level of nutrition and shelter which is biologically determined as the minimum necessary for man to subsist and reproduce his kind. But Marx recoils from such a theory for two reasons: (1) Population changes are too slow to be considered a response to the observable changes in the wage level; (2) The determination of wages at biological subsistence would render all trade union activity by the working class as fruitless as the classical economists had predicted.[17] Marx had assailed the iron law of wages as an attempt to explain low wages and the poverty of the proletarian as a "law of nature" rather than a law of class society in its capitalist stage.[18] In any case, the biological statement of subsistence is simply contrary to fact. If interpreted in this falsifiable way, the subsistence theory would fail in its test.

But Marx also argues that wages are at subsistence by definition.

The value of labour-power is the value of the means of subsistence necessary for the maintenance of the labourer. . . . On the other hand, the number and extent of his so-called necessary wants, as also the modes of satisfying them, are themselves the product of historical development, and depend therefore to a great extent on the degree of civilization of a country, more particularly on the conditions under which, and consequently on the habits and degree of comfort in which, the class of free labourers has been formed. In contra-distinction therefore, to the case of other commodities, there enters into the determination of the value of labour-power an historical and moral element. Nevertheless, in a given country, at a given period, the average quantity of the means of subsistence necessary for the labourer is practically known.[19]

This explanation of subsistence strips the concept of any falsifiable content. The supply schedule of labor merely reflects traditional views as to what an "equitable" going wage is.

Marx qualifies his subsistence theory even further by remarking that "the price of this labour power . . . [is not] given, but only its minimum limit, which is moreover very variable. . . . only in favorable and exceptional cases, has he [the laborer] the power to enlarge the so-called labour-fund at the expense of the 'revenue of the wealthy.' " [20]

At no point could one now possibly test the theory by pointing to a wage level and saying, "This wage is above the subsistence." In effect a supply schedule of labor has been proposed by Marx with shift parameters determined by various conventional views on what is a high or low wage. In reality Marx must concede that wages are determined by supply and demand. All that Marx does here is supply the label *subsistence* to summarize the labor market in any particular nation as shaped by its contingent series of historical events.

While labels do not add to the scientific meaning, the label of subsistence does suggest a low standard of living. This contingent statement about the wage level not only is epistemologically meaningful but, in many places, has been accurate. While it is extraneous to our argument, it is only fair to note that nineteenth-century England was characterized by a level of wages close to biological subsistence. However much one criticizes the rationalism in Marx's argument, it is impossible not to be moved by the condition that he discloses of the working class. Nor would it be honest to ignore the personal character of Marx himself; he devoted his life to ferreting out the data from a mass of official reports and presented them to the public along with his analysis. Marx deserves less blame for mistakenly thinking that the suffering of the factory workers was an inevitable feature of capitalism, than those persons who shut their eyes to the conditions of the "lower classes." However important, these statements are all contingent statements about the status of the worker at any particular time and are dependent on his organization, bargaining power, degree of monopoly, and the like. None of these can be necessarily deduced from the nature of capitalism, and the possibility of the improvement of working-class conditions has become a reality in many nations.

The Demand for Labor and the Dynamic Restatement of Exploitation

Faced with this dilemma Marx in effect revises (in a famous quotation) the subsistence theory by expressing his conviction that through technological and cyclical unemployment the working class will suffer increasing misery. In the long run wages will approach closer and closer to the biological minimum. While the statement is hedged around with qualifications, there seems little doubt that the decline of the labor standard of living was what Marx felt expressed the essence of capitalist evolution:

The greater the social wealth, the functioning capital, the extent and energy of its growth, and, therefore, also the absolute mass of the proletariat and the productiveness of its labour, the greater is the industrial reserve-army. The same causes which develop the expansive power of capital, develops also the labour-power at its disposal. The relative mass of the industrial reserve-army increases therefore with the potential energy of wealth. But the greater is the mass of a consolidated surplus-population, whose misery is in inverse ratio to its torment of labour. The more extensive, finally, the lazarus-layers of the working class, and the industrial reserve-army, the greater is official pauperism. *This is the absolute general law of capitalist accumulation.* Like all other laws it is modified in its working by many circumstances, the analysis of which does not concern us here.[21]

The subsistence theory has been restated in dynamic form. It is not that wages necessarily are *at* subsistence, but they tend downward and are *pressed in the direction* of biological subsistence. The fact that this "general law" is stated as a tendency has made it difficult to test since it is not a prediction which is falsifiable within a specified period of time. As such it has been the subject of much equivocation by Marxists in the face of increasing real labor incomes. In evaluating the law, then, we must concede that in this form it could be considered meaningful provided we were not to allow an indefinite time for its working and allow modifying circumstances to become rationalizations to make it completely untestable. We must consequently examine the basis on which Marx makes the prediction.

The fundamental limitation on wages is to be found in the labor expended as the source of all the value produced. Since the net national product in labor value terms (not *real* terms) is limited by the labor time that the work force can expend, national income cannot grow faster than the natural rate of growth of the laboring population. Here we hold constant the duration and intensity of labor, as well as the process of transfer of labor from noncapitalist enterprises into capitalist production, for example, the enclosure movement in England or the breakup of feudal economies in underdeveloped countries. Consequently, for Marx, the relative division of national income into the proportionate shares of each class tends to take on absolute significance. A relative decline in the *value* share of the working class as a result of the introduction of labor-saving machines tends to be interpreted as resulting in less utility income, for example, "increasing misery." [22] This is not an inevitable outcome of this theory, but it was a conclusion which he often (but not always) assumed.

I have argued in the previous chapter that Marx confused labor expended in supply with demand expressed as a fund. Both of these quantities totaled to the same aggregate value in equilibrium: socially necessary labor time. Since demand and supply are considered as aggregates rather than schedules, Marx thought that, without recourse to using a monetary measure, he could simply add up all the past labor. This became a sum of capital which was the real fund of demand for factors of production—variable and constant capital.

Capital, then, is the amassed value which has fallen into capitalist hands through both "primitive accumulation" and savings of prior exploitation. This fund is then divided between the purchase of labor power and the means of production. [23]

Marx's capital concept is made difficult because he conceives of capital as a mass of "congealed labor" time which may be expressed at one time as a money fund, at another as means of production and labor power, and at still another time as a mass of products available for sale. Only the *form* of capital is metamorphosed however. The circulation of capital is represented by Marx as

$$M - C^L_{Pm} \cdots\cdots C' - M'$$

Here the dash represents exchange of equivalent values. Money (M) is exchanged for the commodities (C), labor power (L), and means of production (Pm). The dots are the production process in which labor power is expended producing commodities of greater value (C') which are transformed into more money capital by exchange (M'). Capital is not the accumulated means of production but rather the total *value* circulated and is limited by the amount of it available. The total employment of factors depends on the volume of only the value aggregate demand, because the price of factors is rigidly determined by their labor value. The more constant capital is employed, the less living labor power will be used.

It is instructive to contrast this account of economic growth with the view of the pre-Keynesian orthodox economist. Growth is limited by the size of the physical plant and equipment, the state of technology, and the size of the labor force. These factors of production are all drawn into action through the price mechanism. They are priced by the market by supply and demand expressed in terms of a money *numéraire*. In the absence of destabilizing income effects on money demand, perverse expectations of future price movements, and monopolistic influences, flexible prices would adjust to the quantity of money and fully employ the factors of production so as to optimally satisfy the demands of the consumers.[24] The rate of interest is the price of savings and reflects the sum of individuals' decisions to consume now or to allocate to the future. The demand schedule for savings, that is, investment, depends on the productivity of capital given the state of technology. The rate of return to savings directed to capital formation declines with the increase of its use because of diminishing returns. Equilibrium is reached when the rate of return on capital equals the interest which must be paid to induce individuals to save.

The Keynesian revolution in economic thought made use of the qualifications of imperfect competition and income effects. In the absence of perfect competition and flexible prices, that is, with sticky money wages and prices, there is no reason to believe that sufficient demand will be forthcoming to maintain full employment. The amount which consumers are able to spend might be less than the potential for manufacturing consumer goods; savings, the residual of income not consumed, might not find a ready made demand in investment. Investment demand might not respond to interest rates but might reflect expectations, rates of change in income and consumption, and the like. Moreover, the interest cost of investment was itself a sticky price because of the desire of individuals to hold money in liquid form, especially in times of stress or panic.

Keynes had euphemistically referred to the consumption-savings decision as the impact of *income* changes on an institutionally determined "propensity" to consume. For short-run pragmatic purposes, during periods of mass unemployment, it might have been possible to argue that the aggregate income effect is more effective for raising demand than the wage-fund versus profit (variable capital and surplus value) division that underlies the propensity.

This may no longer apply at full employment. The process of growth in plant and equipment may be retarded by a high level of real wages which retards savings.[25] Joan Robinson stresses this distributive aspect of the growth problem. But under conditions of full or less than full employment it is not a "value fund" that limits growth in national income investment opportunity. Under conditions of full employment this depends on the physical capital and labor available for production, the wage rate, and the willingness of the capitalist landlord and *rentier* to accumulate rather than consume. During depression it depends more on the demand for consumption and, more strategically, the demand for investment. While consumption and savings depend on the distribution of income in ways which have been neglected by many economists, they are not identical with "last year's" wages or profits. Given the prospects for investment and the willingness to save out of income, the *money* savings are forthcoming. It remains a question whether *real* resources are available. Mrs. Robinson explains the limitation of accumulation by real rather than money resources as follows:

The "supply of investible resources" is no guide, for accumulation generates the savings it requires. The limit to this process is set by the level to which it is possible to force down real wages. In any given state of affairs an upper limit to the possible rate of accumulation is set by the "inflation barrier" which comes into operation when a fall in real wages is being resisted by raising money wages. Short of this limit, the supply of investible resources is whatever is required by the rate of accumulation.

Now does the "supply of loanable funds" provide a clue, for here also the bootstraps operate. A firm which owns capital can pledge it to borrow more. A higher rate of accumulation means a greater flow of profits and so both the greater amount of self-finance and greater borrowing power. The rate of accumulation, below the level set by the tolerable minimum of real wage rates, can be whatever it likes. (This does not, of course, mean that a *rise* in the rate of accumulation in an economy, above what it has been in the past meets no obstacles. It only means that the supply of finance does not prescribe what the normal rate of accumulation must be.) [26]

The nexus between the value-fund theory of effective demand for factors of production and the money demand bears on Marx's monetary theory. To him supply of money capital must correspond to the value fund generated in prior periods. He is forced to reject a quantity theory of money which would adjust the value of total money demand to the volume of commodities to be transacted by adjusting their prices. The quantity theory would leave room for noninflationary flexible expansion of money capital if unemployed real productive factors were available (for example, if the reserve army of unemployment were sizable). [27] Instead Marx substitutes a commodity theory of gold money rigidly valued at its labor content bidding for labor and means of production which are sold as fixed values. A "ghost of gold" theory is provided for representative currency. The supply of money capital must be limited by the previously accumulated mass of value available for accumulation as capital. In plain contradiction to expansion of the money supply by the banks, Marx must have it that if demand is to be available in period two, it must first have been produced in period one, or at some still earlier time, and only now dishoarded.

The limited supply of money capital is the basis for the Marxian reply to Schumpeter's question: Why does not competition among the capitalists reduce surplus value to zero since

ex hypothesi entrepreneurship represents no real cost?[28] Since
in the short run capital is rigidly fixed in supply, competition
among capitalists only involves the redistribution of the surplus
value produced by the workers in proportion to the total capital
advanced. Thus capitalist competition, according to Marx, only
equalizes the rate of profit between industries, not the amount.
Surplus value emerges here as a species of rent resulting from
the rigid supply in the money capital market.[29]

I have suggested that the tendency toward the relative diminution of the demand for variable capital is crucial to Marx's
increasing misery doctrine. But now as capital is accumulated,
will the demand for labor power exceed the natural rate of
growth of the labor force so that surplus value is eliminated by
rising wages? Or will the counteracting forces to wage increases
be so powerful as to increase surplus value?

Marx discusses the means of enlarging surplus value with a
given labor force under the headings of the production of absolute and relative surplus value. By the first of these he means
the attempts of the employers to lengthen the working day or
to increase the intensity of labor for the same variable capital
so that more value is produced for the capitalist. Marx considers
various combinations of increased time, intensity, and skill expended by the workers and gives detailed case histories and
statistics illustrating the exploitation of British labor.[30] Nevertheless, even while he portrays a vivid picture of exploitation,
Marx is quick to add that the increase in absolute surplus value
is limited by the biological necessity to rest at least part of the
twenty-four hours. The inability of a society to maintain a vigor-
ous labor force without meeting minimum standards of subsistence puts a limit on the indefinite extension of this type of
surplus value.[31]

Relative surplus value involves the cheapening of the labor
time necessary for the production of the elements of subsistence
consumed by the working class. Here there is no decline in real
wages (in the sense of a flow of use values to the laborer), but

rather a decline in division of the new product. The rate of surplus value, the amount of surplus value divided by variable capital, rises as a result of a decline in the denominator. Joan Robinson has emphasized that this rise in exploitation may not involve a loss of real wages to the worker. She points out that there is no limit to "The rise in the rate of exploitation which comes about through a rise in productivity, with constant hours and intensity of work, and constant real wages." [32] Usually Marx appears to assume a temporally constant rate of surplus value which expresses the rough balance between the increased wage pressure as accumulation proceeds and the increase in relative surplus value. In particular he needs this for his theory of the declining rate of profit. Mrs. Robinson points out the dilemma that this presents for the rest of Marx's theory.

This proposition stands out in startling contradiction to the rest of Marx's argument. For if the rate of exploitation tends to be constant, real wages tend to rise as productivity rises. Labor receives a constant proportion of an increasing total. Marx can only demonstrate a falling tendency in profits by abandoning his argument that real wages tend to be constant. This drastic inconsistency he seems to have overlooked.[33]

It should be pointed out that Marx was aware of the threat that technological change posed to his doctrine of increasing misery. For instance in *Capital* he says:

The value of labour-power is determined by the value of a given quantity of necessaries. It is the value and not the mass of these necessaries that varies with the productiveness of labour. It is, however, possible that, owing to an increase of productiveness, both the labourer and the capitalist may simultaneously be able to appropriate a greater quantity of these necessaries, without any change in the price of labour-power or in surplus value.[34]

If Marx was aware of the problem for his theory, then we must look further for the basis of the doctrine of increasing misery.

A reconciliation may be attempted by applying the interpretation of value as a demand function rather than a cost determined entity. The value of a unit of a commodity is its aliquot share in the fund of labor which society decides to devote to its production. This decision is expressed as a unit elastic (constant outlay) demand curve. The value of labor power, then, becomes a wages fund and subsistence is the wages fund divided by the number of persons that would be employed at the subsistence value of labor power. In Figure 7 the value of labor power is

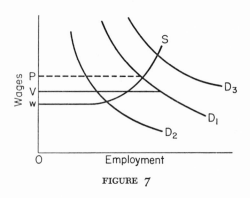

FIGURE 7

indicated by w and the price of labor by P, if the supply is S and D_1 indicates the demand for labor power. Marx indicated the wages fund is "very variable" because, in this interpretation, subsistence is not really an equilibrium price between population and a fixed wages fund. Rather than an iron law of wages Marx has the wages fund as an historically determined *portion* of the capital fund which society on a class-antagonistic basis decides to spend on labor power. In this interpretation we do not determine the size of the wages fund as simply an exercise in arithmetic in which the wage rate established at the margin of supply and demand is multiplied by the number employed. Rather the size of the fund is determined by class conflict, that is, the bargaining strength of the entire proletarian class. This, in part, depends on the demand for labor in light of the technology of the opportunities for substitution of constant capital for labor power; but it depends also on the evolved political and historical determinants of the strength of the laborers and employers. The strategy of the laborers is to move the demand curve from D_1 to D_3, while that of the employers is to move to D_2.

In Figure 7 the supply curve is drawn sloping upward so that the equilibrium wage rate (P) is above its value (w). This is not necessarily true since at low levels of demand for labor the labor force might increase; child and female labor swells the labor force as well as longer hours worked by the male adult proletarians. The price of labor would then be below subsistence wages. If lower wages increase the labor supply, the wage rate might be unstable and move downward indefinitely. If, on the other hand, the supply curve of labor is upward sloping, as it might be if demand is strong, it reflects the higher than value wages of those employed (P). They would receive the value of labor power (V) if they worked longer hours or did not restrict entry into the labor force by a variety of devices ranging from child-labor legislation to restricted union membership. P and V would only be identical if the supply of labor were infinitely elastic.[35]

Holding political factors constant the size of the wages fund turns on the likelihood of an increase in the organic composition of capital, that is, the ratio of the *value* of the constant capital employed (C), to total capital (constant plus variable $C + V$). Marx was convinced that this ratio rose along with accumulation. Note that if the organic composition is constant as well as the rate of surplus value, Mrs. Robinson is right, and increasing productivity means a progressively higher real standard of living for the working class. However, if the organic composition were to increase and if the total amount of capital available to be accumulated were rigidly fixed by past accumulation, then the rise in organic composition implies an absolute diversion of the capital fund from variable to constant, that is, a decline in the wages fund. This decline in variable capital may result in technological unemployment or increased rates of exploitation depending on whether wage rates do decline in the same proportion as capital is shifted from living labor, that is, the net result will depend on the elasticity of supply of labor.

Assuming that the organic increase does not cheapen the final product, it is possible that real wages may decline as well as the rate of surplus value increase in response to the threat of unemployment; but it is equally possible that with increased productivity in consumer goods industries the effect on the labor market might in its impact on real wages and employment be neutral by lowering the value of labor power; or it might even improve real wages and employment as Mrs. Robinson suggests.

An important case for Marx is the one in which dynamic changes do not lower the value of the final product, but simply replace capital accumulated in labor power with accumulation in constant capital. From the viewpoint of the capitalist this is the defensive case. This capital deepening change is a response by capitalists to a rise in wages as the accumulated capital which otherwise must be devoted to labor power as accumulation outstrips the labor supply. Here, neglecting the possibility of introducing or withdrawing hoarded capital into accumulation, a shift to constant capital causes either real wages to fall or unemployment to occur. If the price of labor power is completing an upward movement, *ex hypothesi*, it is more likely, said Marx, that the last possibility would occur. The industrial reserve army of unemployed would swell and wages would be driven down again to the subsistence level. Living labor was seen as in competition with roundabout production by the dead labor which constitutes constant capital. This is the classical means used by the capitalist system to maintain a low level of working-class subsistence and defend its surplus value. If the rate of displacement of living labor by machinery were to exceed the increase in demand for it because of lower wages and secular accumulation of capital, there would be a tendency for the reserve army to increase. But through either unemployment or exploitation at work Marx expected that the working class would be pushed into increasing misery and degradation.[36]

Marx imagined that he had extracted the kernel of truth from the Malthusian argument by turning it into its opposite:

The relative decrease of the variable capital, or the development of the productive power of labor, requires an increasing mass of total capital for the purpose of setting in motion the same quantity of surplus labor. Consequently the possibility of a relative surplus of laboring people develops to the extent that capitalist production advances, not because the productive power of social labor *decreases*, but because it *increases*. Relative overpopulation does not arise out of an absolute disproportion between labor and means of subsistence, or of means for the production of these means of existence, but out of a disproportion due to the capitalist exploitation of labor, a disproportion between the growing increase of capital and its relatively decreasing demand for an increase in population.[37]

The element of truth in Marx's commentary has been pointed out by Mrs. Robinson. *With a given technique* an increased rate of investment of *factors of production* in constant capital, while maintaining full employment, would have to be accomplished at the expense of real wages probably through inflation. But in this case the limitation is the physical labor force and stock of constant capital equipment available. Hence Marx did not adequately consider that as productivity technique advances *pari passu* with investment the barrier to increased real wages is pushed back.

Marx was convinced that the rate of increase in constant capital would exceed that of accumulation as a whole, resulting in the shift into constant capital. He expected that the rate of this shift would exceed the rate of increased productive efficiency in the wage goods industry. To Marx it seemed self-evident that this would be the case. Scattered throughout his work we find passages like the following:

In order that an absolutely increased variable capital may be employed in a capital of higher composition, that is, a capital in which the constant capital has relatively increased still more than the variable the total capital must not only grow in proportion to its higher composition, but even more rapidly. It follows, then, that an even larger quantity of capital is required in order to employ the same, and still more an increased amount of labor-power, to the extent that the capitalist mode of production develops. The increasing productivity of labor thus created necessarily and permanently an apparent overpopulation of laboring people.[38]

Marx's notion that the increased technology will be unable to provide cheaper means of subsistence that might permit lower money wages and increased employment or higher real wages to the employed seems at variance with his panegyrics on the increases in capitalist productivity. Mrs. Robinson's suggestion that Marx simply overlooked the possibility of productivity increases leading to constant or rising real wages does not seem warranted by Marx's comments on the question. But at the same time, he does not appear to give an adequate defense of his apparent view that the effect of such productivity increases are at best temporary in maintaining real wages.

Marx emphasized the distinction between fixed and circulating capital.[39] He pointed out that only the constant capital consumed entered into the value of the product. Consequently, circulating constant capital and the depreciated portion of fixed capital was added to the variable capital and surplus value to make up the final value of the product.

Constant capital consumption compared to total capital might be expected to be relatively stable. One might think of technological improvement in the elements of fixed capital improving their durability which might compensate for the increase in the stock of constant capital being depreciated. Certainly no very clear case can be made here for the increase in constant capital cost in this sense to exceed the increased productivity of consumer goods industries.

It is only plausible to explain Marx in terms of the imposing investments in the total stock of fixed capital he observed as capitalism developed.

It is, of course, conceivable that, given a rigid monetary system which had institutional arrangements prohibiting the development of money substitutes, a limitation on funds available for investment might become effective. Under such circumstances the rate of interest might become high enough to wipe out the net returns to enterprise. But if this is not a completely fanciful condition it is only due to the rigidities of some nineteenth-century monetary systems and has little to do with the inherent capitalist inability to fully employ all the factors of production. Apart from short-run interest expense of liquidity preference, a firm's rate of profit can be capitalized into an acceptable money substitute.

Marx suggested that the process of diversion of capital into constant elements as a result of innovation and wage pressure is also accelerated by the tendency toward monopoly. The concentration of capital into fewer units and its centralization into larger units increases the stock of fixed capital which labor "sets in motion." In a key section of *Capital*, entitled "Relative Diminution of the Variable Part of Capital Simultaneously with the Progress of Accumulation and the Concentration that Accompanies It," Marx concludes:

> The degree of productivity of labour in a given society is expressed in the relative extent of the means of production that one labourer, during a given time, with the same tension of labour-power, turns into products. . . . The increase of some is a consequence, of others a condition of the increasing productivity of labour. . . .
>
> Centralization, by thus accelerating and intensifying the effects of accumulation, extends and hastens at the same time the revolutions in the technical composition of capital, which increase its constant part at the expense of its variable part and thereby reduce the relative demand for labour.[40]

Marx integrates innovation into his oversaving theory of labor misery:

> The masses of capital amalgamated overnight by centralization reproduce and augment themselves like the others, only faster, and thus become new and powerful levers of social accumulation. . . . The additional capitals formed in the course of normal accumulation serve mainly as vehicles for the exploitation of new inventions and dis-

coveries, or of industrial improvements in general. However, the old capital likewise arrives in due time at the moment when it must renew its head and limbs, when it casts off its old skin and is likewise born again in perfected industrial form, in which a smaller quantity of labor suffices to set in motion a larger quantity of machinery and raw materials. The absolute decrease of the demand for labor necessarily following therefrom will naturally be so much greater, the more these capitals going through the process of rejuvenation have become accumulated in masses by the movement of centralization.[41]

Marx was aware of "counteracting causes" in the cheapening of a given machine as its production costs fall. But since he is considering the total industrial plant, the savings in constant capital from this source did not seem likely to be an important factor relative to the total state of technology.

Marx's expectation that increased productivity would not compensate for the reduction of the wages fund is not unrelated to the classical law of diminishing returns. A conclusive argument cannot be made. A possible interpretation of Marx's writing is that he expected that technological improvements producing relative surplus value would become less significant compared to the total stock of capital equipment and in light of the fixed supply of available land. In speaking of the production of relative surplus value, Marx speaks more of the rapid increase in productivity attendant on the drawing of labor into the more efficient capitalist production as opposed to earlier handicraft forms rather than accelerated technological advance. But this is a limited process:

Generally speaking, the specifically capitalist mode of production ceases to be a mere means of producing relative surplus-value, so soon as that mode has conquered an entire branch of production; and still more so, as soon as it has conquered all the important branches. It then becomes the general, socially predominant form of production. As a special method of producing relative surplus-value, it remains effective only, first, in so far as it seizes upon industries that previously were only formally subject to capital [Marx is speaking of the domestic industry or exploitation by mercantile or usurious capital.], that is so far as it is propagandist; secondly, in so far as the industries that have been taken over by it, continue to be revolutionized by changes in the methods of production.[42]

The question then becomes: What limitations are there on methods of production being continually revolutionized? Marx does not really answer. The *total* productivity of labor producing consumer goods is determined both by the inheritance of productive technique and means of production from antiquity and by the fertility and advantages of soil, climate, and the like. Thus he says:

The fewer the number of natural wants imperatively calling for satisfaction, and the greater the natural fertility of the soil and the favourableness of the climate, so much less is the labour-time necessary for the maintenance and reproduction of the producer. So much greater therefore can be the excess of his labor for others over his labor for himself.[43]

A few pages later he goes on to amend this, stating of the natural fertility of the land: "These conditions affect surplus-labour only as natural limits, i.e., by fixing the points at which labour for others can begin. In proportion as industry advances, these natural limits recede." [44]

How flexible are these limits? Marx does not say; but he goes on immediately to discuss Ricardo and John Stuart Mill. He chides Ricardo for assuming instead of discussing the origin of surplus value as a natural category of production. Nevertheless he praises Ricardo for identifying surplus value's increase with that of labor productivity:

Whenever he discusses the productiveness of labour, he seeks in it not the cause of surplus-value but the cause that determines the magnitude of that value. On the other hand, his school has openly proclaimed the productiveness of labour to be the originating cause of profit (read: Surplus value).[45]

Marx thereupon drops the subject. Did he mean to include in his commentary on Ricardo an acceptance of his law of diminishing returns? If so then the increasing labor productivity would be of progressively diminishing significance compared to the increases in organic composition.

However Marx arrived at his conclusion of increasing misery, we must conclude that he failed to see the limitations of his fixed value theory of capital or that he grossly underestimated the ability of capitalism to revolutionize production.

While unemployment and increasing misery are necessary conditions for the preservation of capitalism, the continuation and extension of misery is not unlimited. Trade union resistance, not to speak of biological limitations, prevents the indefinite extension of unemployment and depressed wages. Of equal practical significance is the technological limitation on the short-run marginal substitutability of large amounts of constant for variable capital. Sweezy suggests the possibility that the inability of technological change to keep up with accumulation and consequent wage pressures is the result of the sporadic nature of accumulation which in turn is the result of the unplanned nature of capitalism. He adds a Schumpeterian note: "As capitalism develops sharp fluctuations in the rate of accumulation, partly caused by and partly leading to, technical revolutions become more and more the rule," and wage-saving changes cannot keep up with these bursts of activity and their demand for labor-power.[46]

In other words, it is entirely likely that the accumulation that has to be devoted to variable capital will continue to proceed at a more rapid pace than the extension of the labor supply will. The resultant depletion of the industrial reserve army despite technological innovations will cause higher wages and lower the rate of surplus value. But the static equilibrium of the labor market at full employment is incompatible with profits: since *ex hypothesi* the capitalists perform no service requiring sacrifice under perfect competition they would receive no profit. Schumpeter properly regards the incompatibility of equilibrium in the labor market with the existence of surplus value as evidence of the breakdown of the labor theory of value. Marx, however, sees the incompatibility as the cause of the breakdown of capitalist accumulation. Marx again refers to the reversal of the Malthusian doctrine in this connection:

The law of capitalist production that is at the bottom of the pretended "natural law of population" reduces itself simply to this: The correlation between accumulation of capital and rate of wages is nothing else than the correlation between the unpaid labour transformed into capital and the additional paid labour necessary for the setting in motion of this additional capital. . . . If the quantity of unpaid labour supplied by the working class, and accumulated by the capitalist class, increases so rapidly that its conversion into capital requires an extraordinary addition of paid labour, then the wages rise, and, all other circumstances remaining equal the unpaid labour diminishes in proportion. But as soon as this diminution touches the point at which the surplus labour that nourishes capital is no longer supplied in a normal quantity, a reaction sets in: a smaller part of revenue is capitalized, accumulation lags, and the movement of rise in wages receives a check. The rise of wages is therefore confined within limits that not only leave intact the foundations of the capitalistic system, but also secure its reproduction on a progressive scale.[47]

In other words, given the population and excluding minor counteracting causes, the only basis on which capitalist accumulation can proceed is if the rate of growth of total capital minus the technically feasible accumulation in constant capital is no bigger than the growth of the labor force. The tendency of capital accumulation to outrun this condition once capitalism has destroyed the remnants of earlier forms of production which act as a reservoir of labor-power results, says Marx, in "modern Industry with its decennial cycles and periodic phases." [48]

Here we have the reverse side of the same rigidity in capital concept as we observed where accumulation in constant capital exceeded that necessary to maintain the industrial reserve army. Now all the surplus value produced in the previous period must be invested anew in the next. With no provision for equilibrium between accumulation and rate of return, the process of accumulation must proceed as an exponential function raising the accumulated profit to higher powers as time proceeds, regardless of increasing costs and lower rates of return.

Eventually the mad chase ends, says Marx. "The real barrier of capitalist production is capital itself." [49] The crisis stage of the business cycle serves to reassert this limitation by destroying excess capital in the crash and reducing the wage level by restoring the industrial reserve army of unemployed. Thus:

> The crises are always but momentary and forcible solutions of the existing contradictions, violent eruptions, which restore the disturbed equilibrium for awhile.
> The contradiction, generally speaking, consists in this, that the capitalist mode of production has a tendency to develop the productive forces absolutely, regardless of values and of the surplus-value contained in it. [50]

To Marx the business depression and unemployment is a means of restoring the necessary conditions of increasing misery which could not have been accomplished under full employment. Any objective view of the history of economic thought must give enormous credit to Marx for identifying the self-generating business cycle and for placing it within his system rather than as an externally caused catastrophe. But he cannot at the same time have a balance of the amounts of labor power supplied and demanded at subsistence wages if capital accumulation continues. [51] Nor should the Marxists squirm out of the consequence of the contradictions of their wage theory and the conditions for equilibrium by saying that it is one of the contradictions of capitalism. It should be apparent that the contradictions arise from attempting to apply the meaningless concept of value to the labor bargain.

Conclusions

In the preceding chapter I offered two alternate interpretations of the labor theory of value. The traditional view held that value was a supply concept which identified supply price with the labor expended in the production of a commodity. I argued at that time that if demand were to be ignored as a determinant of the ratio of exchange of commodities supply would have to be infinitely elastic. That is to say the long-run price of a good did not depend on how much of it is being used. While it is doubtful that this condition is met in the price of manufactured goods, it is not possible to maintain this condition in the labor market. The limitation of the size of the labor force implies a rising wage level as the demand for its product grows. If value is conceived of as an equilibrium price it must satisfy the pre-conditions of static equilibrium, equality of *ex ante* supply and demand.[52] If these conditions do not obtain then it is impossible to use the value concept as a long-run price. If the conditions are met then labor power would absorb the whole product. Since capitalists perform no productive function, it would then be meaningless to talk of subsistence wages without either defining "subsistance" away altogether or inventing an artificial limitation on the demand for labor. The dilemma vanishes with a supply and demand theory of labor price and entrepreneurial produc-tivity. The question of the wage bargain then shifts from the rationalist inevitable exploitation theory to both an empirical analysis of the facts and a normative discussion of the changes that the society would like to see made.

The outcome of the labor-value theory of wages is, as we have seen, a shifting of the burden of the problem of subsistence wages to the theory of the business cycle. But the absence of a static equilibrium theory of the value of labor power compatible with profit shows that Marx did not succeed in overcoming the Ricardian dilemma.

If we adopt the suggestion that the value of labor power like that of any other commodity is a statement about the location of a demand curve of unit elasticity, then shifts in the demand curve for labor power is a statement about the size of the wages fund. If the size of the fund is not price (wage) determined but determining, it is likely that it coincides with what Marx meant by the variable and socially determined value of labor power. Wages are not set as a price under competitive conditions, they are determined *by* the wages fund which in turn is the product of class conflict. The wages fund of classical economics may not be a tautology. That is to say wages are not determined on the basis of atomistic decisions of individual workers and capitalists but are the product of group interactions. This amounts to arguing that wages are negotiated on the basis of bilateral monopoly in which a single seller of a commodity confronts a single buyer of it. Let us call the former, the Union, although rightly Marx would be quick to point out that collective bargaining is only one form of class conflict; the buyer can be identified as Capital with equal misgivings about the uniformity of the group and the individuals' relations to the class. But despite the misgiving, there is an air of greater reality about a class bargaining wage contract than one which starts from the labor supply composed of individuals' willingness to work or rest and a demand by atomistic capitalists based on the increase in output they can obtain by hiring an additional employee. Certainly the picture of perfect competition does not correspond to present reality in the Western world. It is likely that it never did, and the quasi-political equivalent of collective bargaining was the case in the last two centuries as well as in this one.

The development of a bilateral analysis of wages has been presented by Kenneth E. Boulding in several places.[53] Let us see if we can adapt his analysis to the Marxian categories.

Net of constant capital consumed and replaced, the value produced (W) in a given period may be considered as equal to the product of the wages fund of variable capital (V) times one plus the rate of value (σ). Since $V = wn$ where (w) is the wage rate and (n) is the number employed, we may write $W = \sigma\, wn$ and $wn = W/\sigma$. In other words, the division of national income into wages fund and capitalists' income depends inversely on one plus the rate of surplus value. Since we can follow Marx in ignoring consumption by the capitalists, the balance of the new value produced can be considered as investment in constant capital. The surplus value produced, in other words, is to be accumulated in either variable or constant capital. Let us define σ' equal to the percent of national income consumed. This is the share of the total product which goes to labor *including additions* to the wages fund.

$$\left(\sigma' = \frac{V + \Delta V}{V + S} = \frac{V + \Delta V}{W}\right)$$

This is equivalent to one minus the portion of the new value produced that goes to investment in *new* constant capital. Since $S = \Delta V + \Delta C$ in this calculation we speak of variable and constant capital after profit has been accumulated so that the share of income remaining the property of the capitalists is the increase in the capital stock. In Marx's diagram we make our measurement at the arrow,

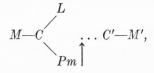

rather than after the process of production indicated by the ellipsis (. . .). Now let us examine Boulding's diagram in Figure 8.[54]

Let each of the indifference curves represented by solid lines show equal levels of satisfaction to the labor movement. They are equally satisfied with the combinations of employment and wage rates illustrated by points on any one of these curves. We need say nothing a priori about the shape of the family of indifference curves other than to require that they be convex toward the origin since both high employment at negligible wages and high wages along with nil employment are less satisfactory than more moderate combinations of w and n. As the indifference curves move toward the right they represent higher levels of satisfaction and labor income. The highest possible such curve would represent labor income which would absorb all of new income W (that is, $\sigma = O$, $\Delta C = O$).

The dotted indifference curves represent a family of curves each of which represents points of equal satisfaction to employers. These start from the upper right-hand corner and move out

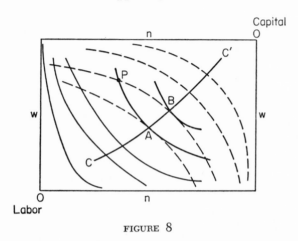

FIGURE 8

toward the left representing greater shares in W. Now if the rate of surplus value at the arrow is equal for all laborers at any given time, then, the unit elastic demand curve is also the locus of equal amounts and rates of return on labor hired by the employers. The employer is indifferent to his position on all points on such a demand curve which represents at once a given size of the wages fund and a value for σ'. If wage rates rise he will hire fewer laborers who will be more skilled or expend more effort so that the rate of exploitation remains the same, or he will do both. A change in the rate of surplus value, and therefore σ' and the wages fund, represents a change in the capitalists' share in the national product and a corresponding change in the labor share. The strategy of labor is to achieve the most satisfactory position by arriving at the highest possible labor indifference curve and thereby reduce the capitalist share.

There is an area in which labor can advantageously trade off wages and employment without necessarily reducing the capitalist share. Such decisions as featherbedding or elimination of child labor and the like can be represented as follows. Suppose initially w and n are at P. Without loss of satisfaction labor could move to position A and at the same time increase the capitalist share. The capitalists at P could equally move to B without loss. In the first case σ' would fall and in the second it would rise. The range AB represents an area of collective bargaining in which both may gain. Thus, from P labor and capital will trade off w and n without loss or essential conflict until they reach the "contract curve," the locus of tangencies of the two systems of indifference curves indicated by CC'. Movement *along* this curve represents changes in σ which alter the well being of capital or labor at the expense of the other.

If wages are determined according to this model of bilateral monopoly we retain the germ of truth in Marx's observation of the wage bargain as one of class bargaining or conflict without the loaded formulation of the epithet "exploitation." It is not that labor is the sole producer of value and is exploited when he does not receive it. Neither is it true that he exists in the fictitious world of perfect competition in which he receives the value of his marginal product and can do nothing by collective bargaining to increase his share without damaging the welfare of the community. The oversimplification we have attributed to Marx in establishing the wages fund by means of a unit elastic demand curve serves to identify the bargaining or "class struggle" and historical aspect of the wage negotiation over relative shares. By making the employer indifferent to the wage rate, given σ', Marx ignores the effect that the equilibrium wage rate has on the size of the fund. The divergence between such a demand curve and other than unit elasticity then might appear to Marx as an error of the second order of smalls which would still preserve a version of the labor theory of value.

In common with all wage-fund theories, the critical issue is how large and how variable is the fund. Clearly in real terms—

as a sum of satisfactions—it is not fixed at all except in the very short run. Higher real wages as a result of increased productivity are entirely possible without shifts in class bargaining powers. However, in terms of the relative share of labor and capital no such flexibility exists. If the concept of value is taken as a share in the national product as we have suggested rather than a long-run price it is likely that when applied to the wage bargain it will be very sticky. The decision by society on the size of the wages fund as the creature of quasi-political bargaining strengths and institutional patterns would not, under normal conditions, be considered as subject to much change. It is widely accepted that this is precisely the pattern in advanced countries. Typically wage shares are strikingly uniform in the history of a given nation, but vary widely between countries.

This chapter, in a sense, has been a recapitaluation of the previous chapter on value. If value is taken—as Marx seemed to say it was—as the ratio which a unit of a good tended to exchange for others, then he is led into insoluble difficulties when he identifies value with labor. The difficulty lifts when value becomes a statement about the division of the national product that society decides to make in producing particular classes of commodities. Really important insights are made by Marx when he follows this line of approach, but the notion of determinacy of the ideal decision-making by material necessity vanishes. Man in society is capable of altering the distribution of wealth, albeit with the use of conflict as well as compromise.

When value is taken as long-run price in the labor market Marx arrives at the notion of subsistence wages which is fraught with contradiction. When subsistence is defined away as a value and becomes a relative share the contradictions disappear along with the label "exploitation." When Marx tries to make his categories absolutes—that is, independent of human volition and alteration—as in the tendency toward subsistence wages and increasing misery, he fails. At the same time his comments on the relative share not only are consistent but serve to encourage the laborer to take advantage of the opportunities to better his lot as opposed to the dismal resignation to poverty envisaged by Malthus and Ricardo.

IV · Crises

The Place of the Business Cycle in Marx's Dynamics of Capitalism: The Absolute Overproduction of Capital

We have seen that the doctrine of the increasing misery of the working class depends on the increasing displacement of living labor power by constant capital. The conditions of low wages and employment are maintained by the rate of accumulation of constant capital exceeding the rate of growth of total capital. With a limited rate of accumulation this might result in a negative growth rate of the variable capital wages fund.[1] Even if this extreme form does not obtain, Marx argued that it still might be the case that more labor power would be thrown on the market than is absorbed with a moderate rate of total accumulation. If we consider wages as the equilibrium price of the value of labor power under conditions of perfect competition this condition is not one of full employment equilibrium. Rather it is a situation of disequilibrium in which an industrial reserve army of unemployed is maintained by replacing the demand for variable capital with that for constant.

Marx considered it more likely that the rate of accumulation would exceed the displacement of labor power and the result would tend toward a no-profit equilibrium. This would be the *tendency* even in the Boulding bilateral monopoly model. It is curious that if variable capital is displaced and the rate of surplus value is held roughly constant, the same fate of increasing misery of the working class would apply to the capitalists as well. One Marxist writer carried this to the absurdity of predicting the end of capitalism through the starvation of the ruling class.[2] Of course Marx made no such predictions, but he did analyze the declining *rate* of profit. Far from expecting the euthanasia of the bourgeoisie Marx was required to explain the rising amount ("mass") of profits within his system.[3] The absolute amount of variable capital must then increase if the amount of surplus value increases and the rate of exploitation is considered almost constant.

"In its working," then, the law of increasing misery of the unemployed "lazarus layers" of society is not operative during period of rapid capital accumulation and a fortiori at full employment. Marx turned to the theory of crises as an integral part of this theory. Fragmentary and incomplete as the posthumously published third volume of *Capital* is, there cannot be much doubt that the discussion of the rate of profit and its tendency to fall and the discussion of underconsumption are aimed at explaining business crises. He returns again and again to the problem, without, however, fully spelling out a theory in a precise causal chain of events. While this is doubtless due in part to the incomplete nature of the work, it is probably also true that, as Dobb and Sweezy suggest, Marx preferred to work by the method of contradiction.

Marx argued, in effect, that increasing misery is the consequence of rapid accumulation, and at the same time "increasing misery" requires the maintenance of an industrial reserve army of unemployed. To the nondialectical theorists "the general law of capitalist accumulation" would be self-contradictory because the continued rapid accumulation of variable capital operates against increasing misery. But to Marx, the general law is an untruth only because in the static analysis the notion of a fixed supply of total capital which might shift from variable to constant is made untrue by accumulation. Accumulation is the constructive negation of static equilibrium. If capital did not grow, it would increase the organic composition at the expense of the unemployment of the laboring class. But accumulation is the "law of Moses and the prophets" to capitalism. This does not cancel out the general law of increasing misery says Marx, the

Hegelian, but now we see how it must operate more particularly through "decennial crises." The theory of crises, the negation of the negation, shows that the process of accumulation is self-contradictory and through them restores the law of increasing misery to operation.

An understanding of this Hegelian type of reasoning in which general laws are subsumed in a synthesis, but not eliminated by a negation, leads to a more accurate interpretation of Marx. He really insisted on the general law of capitalist accumulation despite the "weasel worded" attempt by many Marxists to explain away his statements.[4] At the same time, by use of the dialectic, Marx has characteristically shifted the basis of discussion so that any statistical test of the doctrine of increasing misery is impossible. The doctrine would be held to be true as the inherent tendency of exploitation even though it cannot be tested as a secular trend. As long as accumulation continues and is accompanied by cyclical expansions and contractions, the general law is not falsified. So the theory is true and it is untrue! On one hand it is a denunciation of capitalism, an expression of its essential tendency toward poverty for the masses; on the other, it is a prediction that may not actually ever occur without the theory on which it is based being called to account. The general law is subsumed into another law, that of crisis theory.

The critic stands aghast at the Hydra-headed doctrine which can change a contradiction in the theory of value, that is, in the mind of the dialectical theorist, into a contradiction in the economic real world. Dialectical logic is not required to dispense with a category because it is contradictory at one level of thought.

The law of value, its application, and the equilibrium of supply and demand for labor retains its validity by now becoming interpreted as the *upper limit* of accumulation. Once the total labor force is employed, no more surplus value can be produced unless increasing technological change causes the workers to live on a smaller outlay of variable capital. But given the technology the labor value produced is ultimately limited by the population and the number of hours in a day. Further accumulation can only take place in constant capital which produces no surplus value. Ultimately, at full employment, a point is reached in which the rate of profit $p' = s/(c + v)$ must fall since the numerator is constant and accumulation proceeds by enlarging c in the denominator.

Competition among growing capitals for the limited amount of surplus value results in lower rates of profit to each. Monopolization (centralization) of capital increases as the weakest firms succumb first to the upward tendency in wages. The condition of no increase in total amount of surplus value is the condition of "absolute overproduction of capital." Marx's description is vivid.

There would be an absolute overproduction of capital as soon as the additional capital for purposes of capitalist production would be equal to zero. The purpose of capitalist production is the self-expansion of capital. . . . As soon as capital would have grown to such a proportion compared with the laboring population, that neither the absolute labor time nor the relative surplus-labor time could be extended any further (this last named extension would be out of the question even in the mere case that the demand for labor would be very strong, so that there would be a tendency for wages to rise); as soon as a point is reached where the increased capital produces no larger, or even smaller, quantities of surplus-value than it did before its increase there would be an absolute over-production of capital. That is to say, increased capital $C + \triangle C$ would not produce any more profit, or even less profit, than capital C before its expansion by $\triangle C$. In both cases there would be a strong and sudden fall in the average rate of profit, but it would be due to a change in the composition of capital which would not be caused by the development of the productive forces, but by a rise in the money-value of the variable capital (on account of the increased wages) and the corresponding reduction in the proportion of surplus labor to necessary labor.[5]

The resemblance to contemporary theory of the business cycle is startling![6] In Hicks's model the upswing is the result of the increase in demand for investment in machinery, equipment, and the like. It causes an increase in the demand for all goods and services (national income). The feedback of the further increase in investment demand raises income until the labor force is fully employed. Full employment limits the further growth of output and real income to increases in population and technology. On the upswing of the business cycle, according to Marx, the rate of accumulation of reinvested capital proceeds faster than the natural rate of growth of the labor force. Assuming no consumption by the capitalists, the capital fund in year t, C_t is equal to $(1 + p)C_{t-1}$ where p is the rate of profit; demand for labor power and constant capital equipment in year t is therefore $C_t = C_0 (1 + p)^t$. On the assumption that the rate of profit is greater than the rate of growth of the labor force during the latter phases of the upswing in mature capitalist economies, a ceiling of labor shortage, "absolute overproduction of capital," is eventually reached.

The downswing of the cycle brings out the differences between the Hicks model based on the accelerator and the Marx model of reinvested capital. But there is a similarity in that both require that net investment be negative until the stock of surplus capital is depreciated.

Both models show how the downswing is associated with insufficient consumer demand; a decline in income also reduces consumption demand further reducing income. Underconsumption appears in the Hicks model due to the multiplied reduction in income following from the decline in investment. In the Marxian model the decline in the rate of accumulation results in unemployment. Since consumer demand is identical with laborers' wages in the latter system, the downswing also appears as underconsumption.[7]

The decline in the marginal profit rate to the economy as a whole, argues Marx, does not arrive at a new equilibrium through an equilibrating decline in the rate of accumulation. The puritan ethic of capitalists' drive to accumulate eliminates the possibility of significant consumption of their revenue which would add to consumer demand. Rather the credit system and waves of optimism and panic cause the change in the rate of return on investment to be accompanied by cataclysm and contradiction rather than continued development along a slower warranted rate of growth. The situation is made worse, because as the amount and rate of profit fall, monopoly provides an inertia continuing investment beyond rational limits. Accumulation by large firms may continue at the expense of the smaller and presumably less efficient firms. Says Marx:

> there comes a certain limit where large capital with a small rate of profit accumulates faster than small capital with a large rate of profit. This increasing concentration in its turn brings about a new fall in the rate of profit at a certain climax. The mass of the small divided capitals is thereby pushed into adventurous channels, speculation, fraudulent credit, fraudulent stocks, crises.[8]

Marx is on solid empirical ground in his description of the prelude to the financial collapse. But by the same token these valuable insights into the workings of unrestricted nineteenth-century capitalism are not a logically necessary characteristic of any capitalist society. Of course there is no guarantee that the regulatory and central banking authorities will have the skill or political authority to avoid the speculative excesses Marx describes.

Nevertheless, even if overexpansions of credit are avoided, the existence of fixed intercapitalist obligations and the decline in the profit rate bring the process of accumulation to an end. An interest rate required to overcome the desire of the capitalists to hold their assets in money or near money form may lead to secular stagnation,[9] or it might result in the catastrophic financial panic that was familiar to Marx as the concomitant of the downturn of the business cycle. Marx vividly describes such a collapse:

> the process of reproduction is based on definite assumptions as to prices, so that a general fall in prices checks and disturbs the process of reproduction. This interference and stagnation paralyzes the function of money as a medium of payment, which is conditioned on the development of capital and the resulting price relations. The chain of payments due at certain times is broken in a hundred places, and the

disaster is intensified by the collapse of the credit-system. Thus violent and acute crises are brought about, sudden and forcible depreciations, and actual stagnation and collapse of the process of reproduction, and finally a real falling off in reproduction.[10]

In the end the crisis cures itself. Total accumulation becomes negative and the basis for later capital accumulation is restored:

The principal work of destruction would show its most dire effects in a slaughtering of the *values* of capitals. That portion of the value of capital which exists only in the form of claims on future shares of surplus-value or profit, which consists in fact of creditor's note on production in its various forms, would be immediately depreciated by the reduction of the receipts on which it is calculated. One portion of the gold and silver money is rendered unproductive, cannot serve as capital. One portion of the commodities on the market can complete its process of circulation only by means of an immense contraction of its prices, which means a depreciation of the capital represented by it. In the same way the elements of fixed capital are more or less depreciated. . . . The stagnation of production would have laid off a part of the laboring class and thereby placed the employed part in a condition in which they would have to submit to a reduction of wages even below the average. This operation has the same effect on capital as though the relative or absolute surplus-value had been increased at average wages.[11]

Capital would be destroyed and population increases which took place in the boom would now add to the relative labor surplus. With lower wages accumulation of capital would begin on a larger scale.

Thus, says Marx, "The present stagnation of production would have prepared an expansion of production later on within capitalist limits. And in this way the cycle would be run once more." [12] Marx, it will be noted, has a great deal of difficulty in destroying the surplus capital. To be sure he can destroy constant capital physically through depreciation and obsolescence. But this is a slow process and in any case it is the *value* which is to be destroyed. Further, *all value* is to be depreciated, not just that embodied in constant capital. Yet all Marx can say is that resources or money are temporarily idle due to insufficient compensation. Marx must have them destroyed so that capital can painstakingly be recreated in accumulation under conditions of excess labor power relative to capital. But neither gold nor money is physically destroyed, nor do they lose their relative values compared to the lowered price of labor power. The destruction of the value of claims on surplus value in the form of a credit collapse is real enough. But the very ease with which these claims may be depreciated is testimony to the fact that they can just as easily be revived on the basis of anticipated income. As I have argued, once Marx has created a metaphysical capital substance which lies beyond experience, he finds that it is impervious to destruction by means arising from the world of reality.[13]

According to Marx capital meets impassable limits in attempting to expand national income measured in the labor value of its products. Now it would be ridiculous for the critics of Marx to argue that capital accumulation does not face limits; but these limits are made unduly rigid, as Joan Robinson points out, by Marx's habit of "reckoning in values" rather than in physical terms. Given the labor force, labor value cannot increase at full employment; but, with greater productivity, income in physical and utility terms can. The Marxist Gillman in commenting on Robinson's remark retorts that one might reckon in physical units but then it would not be Marxism which turns on the labor theory of value. But this is just the point. It is the very rigidity of the labor theory of value which precludes economic growth by technological deepening and progress with full employment at a rate exceeding the population growth. It is precisely this "iron law of national income" that neglects the growth in physical terms which results from increasing productivity.

The Trend of Crises and the Decline in the Rate of Profit

The "absolute overproduction of capital" account of crises has two drawbacks from Marx's point of view. Firstly, it postpones

a crisis until absolute full employment is reached. Such absolute
overproduction of capital may in fact rarely be attained, and in
fact a downturn in business activity characteristically occurs
long before such an extreme position is attained. Secondly, and
more important, Marx's crisis theory is part of his intention to
demonstrate the workings of the theory of *increasing* misery of
the working class. The mere repetition of the business cycle was
not enough; he had to show the increasing susceptibility of
capitalism to progressively more severe crises. In the words of
The Communist Manifesto:

> Crises . . . by their periodical return put the existence of the entire
> bourgeois society on trial, each time more threateningly. . . . The
> productive forces at the disposal of society no longer tend to further
> the development of the conditions of bourgeois property; on the con-
> trary, they have become too powerful for these conditions, by which
> they are fettered, and no sooner do they overcome these fetters than
> they bring disorder into the whole of bourgeois society. . . . And
> how does the bourgeoisie get over these crises? On the one hand by
> enforced destruction of a mass of productive forces; on the other, by
> the conquest of new markets, and by the more thorough exploitation
> of the old ones. That is to say, by paving the way for more extensive
> and more destructive crises, and by diminishing the means whereby
> crises are prevented.[14]

Marx's expectation of a progressive deterioration of the capitalist economy through crises is unmistakable.[15]

The argument for the tendency toward more severe crises is
contained in the famous theory of the tendency for the rate of
profit to decline.[16] Here Marx argues that given the rate of
surplus value as a parameter of the relative bargaining strengths
of the capitalist and working classes and the tendency for the
accumulation of capital to increase the organic composition of
capital, the rate of profit would tend to decline, that is, the
denominator of $p' = s/(c + v)$ rises faster than the numerator.
Thus, the total mass, that is, amount, of surplus value may rise
as a result of more variable capital being employed, but, since

the constant capital rises faster than the variable, the rate of profit falls. Following Sweezy's formulation we can write:[17]

$$p' = \frac{s}{c+v} = \left(\frac{s}{v}\right)\left(\frac{v}{c+v}\right).$$

Let $s/v = s'$, the rate of surplus value; $v/(c+v) = q'$; where $1 - q' = q$ the organic composition of capital, $c/(c+v)$. Then $p' = s'q'$ and a rise in organic composition with a given value for the rate of surplus value causes a decline in the profit rate.[18]

All of this is purely analytic. The real question turns on two matters of fact: (1) Does the organic composition of capital increase? (2) Is the rate of surplus value constant? These questions have a familiar ring because they are the same problems discussed in connection with the absolute amounts of variable capital and surplus value analyzed in the previous chapter. Much of the confusion about what *tendency* means to Marx turns on the meaning of "increasing organic composition of capital" and the ambiguity of the flow-and-stock approaches in his writing. In the discussion of the declining rate of profit the ambiguity arises from Marx's calculation of arithmetic illustrations of the law on the assumption of all the constant capital employed being consumed in each turnover of capital, that is, fixed capital is treated as zero.

It seems evident that this was a mere arithmetic convenience. In all the preceding chapters of Volume III of *Capital*, Marx calculates the profit rate on the total capital. Marx says as much:

The magnitude of the actual value of the product of this capital depends on the magnitude of the fixed part of the constant capital, and on the amount of it passing by wear and tear over to the product. But as this circumstance is immaterial so far as the rate of profit and the present analysis are concerned, we assume for the sake of simplicity that the constant capital is transferred everywhere uniformly and entirely to the annual product of the capitals named.[19]

Marx takes pains to make the point clear that he was making a computational simplification:

Before passing on to something new, we will, for the sake of preventing misunderstanding, repeat two statements, which we have substantiated at different times. . . . The same process, which brings about a cheapening of commodities in the course of development of the capitalist mode of production, also causes a change in the organic composition of the social capital invested in the production of commodities, and thereby lowers the rate of profit. We must be careful, then, not to confound the reduction in the relative cost of an individual commodity including that portion of its cost which represents wear and tear of machinery, with the relative rise in the value of the constant as compared to the variable capital.[20]

In other words Marx probably realized at this juncture that there was no reason to believe that the constant capital *consumed* will rise in value terms. Consequently, the rate of profit calculated in flow terms need not fall. Indeed the fact that it does not fall is the burden of Gillman's conclusions working with U.S. National Income statistics. Rather it appears that Marx meant just what he said when he argued that the denominator of the profit rate was the mass of total capital stock "set in motion":

The gradual and relative growth of the constant over the variable capital must necessarily lead to *a gradual fall of the average rate of profit,* so long as the rate of surplus value, or the intensity of exploitation of labor by capital, remain the same. Now we have seen that it is one of the laws of capitalist production that its development carried with it a relative decrease of variable compared with constant capital, and consequently as compared to the total capital which it sets in motion.[21]

It seems to me that a careful reading of Marx's more cryptic statements on the subject reveal at least a consistency with the stock point of view.[22] The stock approach is consistent also with Sweezy's (Keynesian) reading of the declining rate of profit, by making the profit rate (rather the profits of "enterprise") on the total stock of capital related to the interest on total capital extracted from the industrial capitalists by the money capitalists. The sticky interest claims of this latter *rentier* class are thus seen by Sweezy as one of the tendencies toward stagnation. Most important, the stock point of view is consistent with Marx's apparent belief in the long-run ineffectiveness of the "cheapening of the elements of constant capital" as a counteracting cause to the declining profit rate. It is the whole mass of constant capital which inevitably tends to increase, not its depreciated portion. Given this Marx is certainly on plausible ground when he says that only "in exceptional cases the mass of the elements of constant capital may even increase, while its value remains the same or falls." [23] But if the depreciation-flow version of the declining profit rate cannot really demonstrate that an increase in organic composition occurs the approach which relies upon changes in the stock of constant capital must at best be a slow secular tendency. On this view the declining profit rate cannot serve as an immediate cause of crisis. It is true that it might still be possible that a secular decline might lead to either stagnation or more severe crises when they do break out. But if this is the time allotted for the decline to appear one must question whether in the long run the rate of surplus value will always be constant. Is it not just as likely that the exploitation rate will be increased as well? May not the rate of profit be increased by technological change? Sweezy feels the force of this argument and agrees that, a priori, the future of the profit rate is indeterminate.

Indeed one may ask if the capitalist computes his rate of return in percentage of capital advanced or in relation to his costs including the interest cost of borrowing that capital. In the second case, assuming a flexible long-run money supply free from artificial restriction, there is no reason why even a low profit rate on the *stock* of fixed capital (perhaps associated with a large *mass* of profit) should result in a crisis as long as it exceeds the minimum "liquidity trap" interest rate. An *individual firm* might face difficulties of declining profit rate on its stock of capital if the fixed investments were excessive. But this merely expresses that its interest charges exceed the average because its fixed plant was more than average. The equilibrium for the economy as a whole need not behave in the same way. As long as an adequate return on the *costs* of the firm including the depreciated fixed capital can be maintained, expansion can continue up to the margin of the willingness of the public to lend. Marx's system implicitly leaves room for this interpretation in considering interest as a subdivision of surplus value. Marx argues that while short-run interest rates might threaten the profits of enterprise, in the long run, the interest rates must follow the downward trend of the rate of profit.

In an attempt to rescue the declining rate of profit theory from these objections and from the statistical evidence which he himself advances, Gillman resorts to the device of subtracting merchandising costs from the numerator of the profit formula. Marx had included distribution costs other than transportation in the category of surplus value. Since the labor expended in circulation of commodities including its sale and financing do not involve the physical battle of man against nature they were not productive and had to be paid for out of surplus value. It is, of course, true that there may *very well* be an increase in the overhead costs of distribution which make for greater susceptibility to depression. These fixed costs, like the other increased overhead costs of mature capitalism, do add rigidity to the system. But they do not specify an absolute restrictive limit to accumulation which cannot be overcome by technological change. In some respects the increased costs of distribution might be the result of technological change as it represents itself in increased specialization in both consumer and producer markets.

Maurice Dobb has attempted to defend the theory by arguing that the technological changes increasing the organic composition are likely to be of the defensive type associated with the upswing of the business cycle; the closer we get to absolute overproduction of capital, the greater will be the increases in organic composition aimed at merely maintaining the going rate of surplus value. As Gillman would have it the decline in the rate of profit is not the cause of the cycle but its result.[24] Both writers have considerable backing from Marx in his discussion of absolute overproduction of capital. Marx argues that with the total utilization of the labor force the only area in which accumulation can proceed is in constant capital. This accumulation by increasing the organic composition is also a response to increased wage pressures threatening the rate of surplus value. Dobb calls these technological changes intensive as opposed to extensive accumulation of constant capital which lowers the value of the final product.[25]

Insofar as Dobb's view is merely a repetition of the absolute overproduction of capital discussion it shares its weaknesses of underestimating the possibility of extensive technology and its failure to establish any secular trend for the profit rate. The only saving aspect of this interpretation would be to argue that there is a residuum of new constant capital that is not destroyed by the crisis which succeeds the boom and which continues to add to the base of capital stock used for the calculation of the profit rate. But surely such a residuum would be of the same order of magnitude as the long-run increases in the rate of surplus value brought about by the technological change. A cyclical interpretation of the rate of profit theory neglects the fact that the crisis tends to wring out inefficient firms and techniques as well as lower inflated wages. It thus serves to raise long-run productivity and increase the rate of surplus value. One could equally well derive a cyclical theory of the increase in the profit rate through the relative and absolute production of surplus value.

Underconsumption as an Independent Cause of Crises

Sweezy is obviously dissatisfied with the declining rate of profit explanation. Very likely he is struck by Robinson's thrust which demonstrates the increased real income of the working class with a constant rate of surplus value. Accordingly he attempts a reconstruction of the underconsumptionist element in Marx's crisis theory. This has been a moot point among Marxist economists for many years.

The extreme position was taken by Rosa Luxemburg in *The Accumulation of Capital* in 1913.[26] The then powerful socialist parties of Western Europe were committed to a program of direct labor action to end the world war that was imminent. Yet as the international crisis deepened it was clear that the Second International would split between those who would denounce the conflict as an imperialist war and those of each nation who would regard the struggle as the "defense of the fatherland." As a leader of the German left-wing (Spartacus) socialists, Luxemburg wrote to explain that the war was the product of imperialism. Despite the fact that she couched her argument in the abstract terms of the Marxian reproduction schemes her intent was to show that underconsumption was an inevitable and increasingly threatening aspect of capitalism. She argued that capitalist nations must search for markets outside the orbit of advanced capitalist countries to avoid crises. What ensued was the world-wide struggle for the division and redivision of world markets resulting in world wars. Lenin's evaluation of her reveals how far from the abstract her thinking was:

Sometimes eagles may fly lower than hens, but hens can never rise to the height of eagles. Rosa Luxemburg was mistaken on the question of the independence of Poland; . . . she was mistaken on the theory of the accumulation of capital. . . . But in spite of her mistakes she was—and remains for us—an eagle. . . . "After August 4, 1914, German Social-Democracy is a stinking corpse"—this is the utterance which will make Rosa Luxemburg's name live forever in the history of the world working-class movement.[27]

Lenin's own analysis of imperialism seems more consistent with the declining rate of profit theory and the absolute overproduction of capital. In his *Imperialism, The Highest State of Capitalism* the growth of monopoly becomes important enough (presumably the organic composition of capital becomes correspondingly large although Lenin does not discuss it here) to make the export of the "superfluity of capital" to underdeveloped areas both possible and necessary.[28] This emphasis would have imperialism only secondarily concerned with developing a market in the colonial countries but would emphasize the employment of cheap labor with low organic compositions of capital necessary for their employment. Monopoly would concentrate on the extractive industries, transport, and would enforce restrictions of industrialization which would compete with the home country. Imperialism, said Lenin, does not undermine the precapitalist social forms of the underdeveloped countries but restricts its activities to those which can utilize the low wage standards which they imply. Needless to say, Lenin's analysis certainly is relevant to nineteenth-century imperialism, but its inevitability is hitched to the declining rate of profit thesis and the consequent impossibility of continued capitalist accumulation on a world basis.

Rosa Luxemburg's analysis has it that capitalism cannot exist at all without an "external market" of the noncapitalist world. As the colony is drawn into capitalist production, the more the colony becomes subject to the laws of capitalist development and the less it is able to consume. Luxemburg's thesis implies that as capitalism spreads in underdeveloped nations trade between it and the developed areas should decline, but the *facts* exactly contradict this analysis. Sweezy argues that an external market can add nothing to the net consuming power of the imperialist country for an indefinite period of time since the balance of payments problem prevents continuing unilateral imports by the colonies.[29] It is possible, however, that the balance of payments might be redressed by the acquisition of assets in colonial countries. If this were the case, the unrequited imports of the colonies, might be the other side of the coin of the exports of capital from the metropolis.

Luxemburg's attempts to derive underconsumption from the reproduction schema of Marx in Volume II of *Capital* only really illustrate the necessary conditions for continued circulation of commodities. Most writers, Marxists included, have taken them as a description of the actual circulation of capital as well. Marx explains that the circulation has to be interrupted to explain the crisis, but this is not to be seen by the process of circulation described as the necessary conditions for its continued working.

These schema may be algebraically summarized by allowing C to represent constant capital consumed, V is variable capital consumed, and S is surplus value produced in one turnover of capital.

Let W_1 be the value of product of department I, producer goods, and W_2 that of department II, consumer goods. Then

$$W_1 = C_1 + V_1 + S_1$$
$$W_2 = C_2 + V_2 + S_2.$$

If there is simple reproduction the necessary conditions of equality of supply and demand for consumer goods is

$$W_2 = C_2 + V_2 + S_2 = V_2 + S_2 + V_1 + S_1$$
or
$$C_2 = V_1 + S_1.$$

If there is expanded reproduction (accumulation) then S is divided into three parts: α equals percentage of accumulation devoted to variable capital; β equals percentage of accumulation devoted to constant capital; γ equals percentage of surplus value consumed by capitalists. Then, if the rate of surplus value $(S/V) = \sigma'$, we obtain

$$W_1 = C_1 + V_1 + \alpha\sigma'V_1 + \beta\sigma'V_1 + \gamma\sigma'V_1$$
$$W_2 = C_2 + V_2 + \alpha\sigma'V_2 + \beta\sigma'V_2 + \gamma\sigma'V_2.$$

To equate supply and demand for consumer goods, let

$$W_2 = C_2 + V_2 + \alpha\sigma'V_2 + \beta\sigma'V_2 + \gamma\sigma'V_2$$
$$= V_2 + \alpha\sigma'V_2 + \gamma\sigma'V_2 + V_1 + \alpha\sigma'V_1 + \gamma\sigma'V_1,$$

or the necessary condition is

$$C_2 + \beta\sigma'V_2 = V_1 + \alpha\sigma'V_1 + \gamma\sigma'V_1.$$

In Volume II Marx has abstracted from all the dynamic tendencies of the economy. Consequently, the *ceteris paribus* of these forms extends to the absence of shifts of capital from one department to another, from the influence of the credit system and the nature of money, and from deviations of price from value.

Rosa Luxemburg sketches these necessary conditions in arithmetic form. Somehow she produces the notion that department I "takes the initiative" in determining the rate of accumulation. (Joan Robinson points out that mutually determining quantities are completely neutral, and hence for equilibrium nothing need show any initiative.) Luxemburg continues as follows:

It is the very essence of accumulation that capitalists refrain from consuming a part of their surplus value which must be ever increasing— at least as far as absolute figures are concerned—that they use it instead to make goods for the use of other people. It is true that with accumulation the personal consumption of the capitalist class will grow and that there may even be an increase in the total value consumed; nevertheless it will still be no more than a part of the surplus value that is used for the capitalists' abstention from consuming the whole of their surplus value. But what of the remaining surplus value, the part that is accumulated? For whom can it be destined? According to Marx's diagram, Department I has the initiative: the process starts with the production of producer goods. And who requires these additional producer goods? The diagram answers that Department II needs them in order to produce the means of consumption in increased quantities. Well then, who required these additional consumer goods? Department I, of course—replies the diagram—because it now employs a greater number of workers. We are plainly running in circles. From the capitalist point of view it is absurd to produce more consumer goods, merely in order to keep this surplus of workers occupied. Admittedly, as far as the individual capitalist is concerned, the worker is just as good a consumer . . . but who can buy the products incorporating the other, the capitalized part of surplus value? Partly the capitalists themselves—the diagram answers—who need new means of production for the purpose of expanding production, and partly the new workers who will be needed to work . . . there must have been a new demand for the productions which are to be turned out.[30]

In this amazing statement Rosa Luxemburg seems to conclude that expanded reproduction is in contradiction with its own necessary conditions. Why we would ask should not the circulation of capital "run in circles"?

Of greater importance than her own demonstration (which really proves too much, that is, that capitalism is flatly impossible) is Rosa Luxemburg's rebuttal to Tugan-Baranowsky's criticism of underconsumptionism. She declares that both he and Marx err in suggesting that even with limited consumption accumulation should continue by greater investment in the elements of constant capital. She argues that the purpose of production is consumer goods and that Tugan-Baranowsky's ideas ignore this reality of economic life.

The temptation for the Marxists to seize on underconsumption as an explanation of crisis is easy to see. It would afford a plain and direct connection between exploitation and the breakdown of capitalism. It would also provide a political link between the trade union demands for higher wages and the petty bourgeoisie who are ruined in the course of a depression.

Paul M. Sweezy, the leading American Marxist, attempted a demonstration in 1942 which is based upon two fundamental notions: (1) the rate of growth of consumption divided by the rate of growth of means of production declines while (2) the rate of growth of output of consumption goods to the rate of growth of means of production, remains constant.[31] As accumulation proceeds, Sweezy argues, the increase in means of production implies a greater output of consumer goods by (2) and consequently overproduction in the light of limited consumer demand by (1). He supplements this argument with a mathematical appendix.

Sweezy's presentation has been subject to damaging criticism, particularly by Evsey D. Domar, one of the pioneers of growth theory in contemporary economic thought. Domar is willing to provisionally accept a fixed relationship between means of production and output, but points out that this is not the same as Sweezy's ratio (2). It may be that as Marx thought likely a greater portion of the national product goes to investment in constant capital, Domar concedes, "But from this we cannot yet conclude that *capital* will grow faster than income . . . the fact that one function (investment) grows faster than another (income) does not necessarily mean that the integral of the first function (i.e., capital) must grow faster than the second function itself." [32] Referring to an earlier demonstration which he made Domar continues, "It can be shown that if income grows at the rate of r percent per unit of time (year), and if α percent of it is annually invested, the ratio of capital to income will approach as a limit the expression α/r where α and r need not necessarily be constant." [33] Domar then corrects Sweezy's mathematical translation of the verbal argument. He shows that Sweezy could have made his argument stronger by comparing percentage *rates* rather than amounts of growth of investment in constant capital and consumption relative to income. [34] Nevertheless, accumulation can proceed without underconsumption if the *increase* of demand for consumption goods and means of production is large enough to induce a full employment level of investment. This may be the case even though the amount of investment in constant capital desired by the capitalists is an increasing ratio to consumption (or income). Now the requirement for the increase in consumption to suffice is that it increases by increasing amounts or that the second derivative over time be positive. But this condition is satisfied by any exponential growth curve no matter how modest, so long as the base of the growth function is greater than one. [35] The *rate* of growth r need only increase if, or to the extent that, α does so that accumulation may proceed.

It should be noted, as Domar does, that by pointing out the necessary or warranted conditions for continued reproduction does not insure that these will be achieved. Neither does it imply that these conditions are sufficient for continued accumulation. It is therefore by no means evident that the warranted rate of growth must be maintained. Once the pace falters then demand for investment slackens and all the symptoms of underconsumption and insufficient demand appear. It seems to me that Marx's own utterances have been aimed at this point rather than meant as demonstrations that underconsumption is inevitable. Given the anarchy of capitalist production Marx felt that the delicate balance required would not be likely to be maintained.

The delicacy of the balance required is, of course, provided by the fixed relationship between capital in the form of means of production and output. This concept has been the subject of considerable criticism by economists.

An excellent criticism of the concept of a fixed accelerator as a tool of long-run growth analysis has been provided by Solow. He shows that the price mechanism can, at full employment, adjust the capital-output ratio to the production function and the "natural" rate of growth of the labor force. Consequently, the instability of the system which would result from even a slight deviation from the warranted rate of growth is a lot less than Domar imagined.[36]

The actual burden of Marx's remarks are characteristically aimed at Say's law of markets, which denied the possibility of crises. He speaks of it as "the childish babble of a Say . . . not worthy of Ricardo" when the latter accepts it as part of his doctrine. In a typical passage Marx says:

If for example purchase and sale, or the movement or metamorphosis of commodities, represent the unity of two processes—or rather the course of a single process through two opposite phases, and thus in essence the unity of the two phases—this movement is nevertheless, equally in essence, the separation of the two phases, making them independent of each other. Since in fact they belong together, the independence of the two linked phases can only show itself forcibly, as a destructive process. It is precisely the *crisis* in which their unity asserts itself—the unity of different things. The independence in relation to each other which is assumed by these mutually dependent and complementary phases, is forcibly destroyed. The crisis therefore makes manifest the unity of the phases which have become independent of each other. No crisis would take place, were it not for this inner unity of what on the surface are phases unrelated to each other. But no!— says the apologist economist. Because there is unity there can be *no* crisis. Which in turn is nothing but to say that the unity of opposites excludes their antagonism.[37]

In a striking anticipation of what has since come to be known as Walras' Law,[38] Marx says:

That only *particular* but not *all* kinds of commodities can constitute a glut in the market, and that consequently overproduction can always be partial, is a paltry evasion. . . . What is involved here is precisely the moment of crisis. In fact, all commodities (may be in oversupply) except *money*. The necessity for the *commodity* to transform itself into money means only that the necessity exists for *all* commodities.[39]

Overproduction then is a feature of the crisis. But what brings the crisis about is another matter entirely. Certainly underconsumption of the working class *might* bring about the crisis in a particular circumstance in which the requisite balance for a warranted rate of growth were not achieved. The closest Marx comes to underconsumption as an independent explanation apart from the general notion of anarchy of capitalist production is in the following passage quoted by Sweezy, which I quote in full:

The creation of this surplus-value is the subject of the direct process of production. As soon as the available quantity of surplus-value has been materialized in commodities, surplus-value has been produced. But this production of surplus-value is but the first act of the capitalist process of production, it merely terminates the act of direct production. Capital has absorbed so much unpaid labor. With the development of the process, which expresses itself through a falling tendency of the rate of profit, the mass of surplus-value thus produced is swelled to immense dimensions. Now comes the second act of the process. The entire mass is to reproduce the constant and variable capital, as well as a portion representing surplus-value, must be sold. If this is below the prices of production, the laborer has been none the less exploited, but his exploitation does not realise as much for the capitalist. It may yield no surplus-value at all for him, or only realise a portion of the produced surplus-value, or it may even mean a partial or complete loss of his capital. The conditions of direct exploitation and those of the realisation of surplus-value are not identical. They are separated logically as well as by time and space. The last named power is not determined either by the absolute productive power or by the absolute consuming power, but by the consuming power based on antagonistic conditions of distribution, which reduced the consumption of the great mass of the population to a variable minimum within more or less narrow limits. The consuming power is furthermore restricted by the tendency to accumulate, the greed for an expansion of capital and a production of surplus-value on an enlarged scale.[40]

The reader will note that in this expression Marx is only presenting the possibility of crises of underconsumption. But when it comes specifically to a question of a determinate, causal theory of crisis, Marx is explicit. In his famous retort to Rodbertus (also quoted by Sweezy) he rejects the underconsumption thesis and stresses the symptomatic nature of the problem of realization of commodities:

It is purely a tautology to say that crises are caused by the scarcity of solvent consumers, or of a paying consumption. The capitalist system does not know any other modes of consumption but a paying one, except that of the pauper or of the "thief." If any of the commodities are unsaleable, it means that no solvent purchasers have been found for them, in other words, consumers (whether commodities are bought in the last instance for productive or individual consumption). But if one were to attempt to clothe this tautology with a semblance of the profounder justification of their own product, and the evil would be remedied by giving them a larger share of it, or raising their wages, we should reply that crises are precisely always preceded by a period in which wages rise generally and the working class actually gets a larger share of the annual product intended for consumption. From the point of view of the advocates of "simple" (!) common sense, such a period should rather remove a crisis. It seems, then, that capitalist production comprises certain conditions which are independent of good or bad will and permit the working class to enjoy that relative prosperity only momentarily, and at that always as a harbinger of a coming crisis.[41]

Finally, even when (in opposition to Say's Law) Marx is at pains to express the possibility of a crisis due to insufficient consumer demand, he discusses it as one of the contradictions of the declining rate of profit. It is one of the cumulative causes of the downturn precipitated by the absolute overproduction of capital. He takes care to remark that the possibility does not constitute a causal theory of crisis. Thus after discussing the possibility of sales without subsequent purchases which is a "contradiction inherent in money as a means of payment," he goes on to say:

But these also are mere forms, general possibilities of crises; and consequently also forms, abstract forms, of actual crisis. In them the nature of crisis appears in its simplest forms, and, insofar as this form is itself its simplest content, in its simplest content. But it is not as yet a content which is a *determinate cause*. The simple circulation of money and even the circulation of money as a means of payment—and both make their appearance long *before* capitalist production, without crises occurring—are possible and in fact take place without crises. On the basis of these forms alone, therefore, it is not possible to explain why they show their critical side, why the contradictions contained in them as a possibility emerges as a real contradiction.[42]

The need for deepening crisis is included in Marx's increasing misery theory of wages. Yet Marx cannot provide us with an adequate theory. But the contradictions inherent in the wage bargain as Marx saw it can only be resolved by crisis. Marx is convinced that the contradictions will *find a way* to vent themselves in crisis and therefore crises are a logical consequence of capitalism. But the logical necessity is purely of the dialectical variety. In the end the crisis is a particular expression of the dialectical notion of capitalism as a system which, by developing, must destroy itself. The particular causation is a problem of the Understand—of the science of cause and effect.[43]

Crises and Dialectics

Though Marx might not satisfy us with an adequate theory in the realm of the scientific Understanding, he feels that the contradiction is cause enough. The actual causes may be provided through further development of the Understanding of political economy (Marx was sure he was on the right track with his theory of declining rate of profit); or the causes may be entirely particular to each crisis—underconsumption, monetary distress, credit inflation, and the like. But these are the particular forms. The necessity stands above all these as the content, which is the preservation of the system of exploitation by maintaining and increasing the misery of the exploited proletariat.

All this seemed as self-evident to him as it does seem an unwarranted rationalist presupposition to us. Marx says:

We can see how great is the stupidity of economists who, when they are no longer able to reason out of existence the phenomenon of overproduction and crisis, soothe themselves by saying that only the possibility of crises is given in these forms [that is, money and the circulation of commodities] and that therefore their emergence is *accidental*, and so the advent of crisis itself is a mere *accident*.

The contradictions developed in the circulation of commodities, and further development in the circulation of money—and the consequent possibilities of crisis—reproduce themselves spontaneously in capital inasmuch as the developed circulation of commodities and circulation of money in fact arise only on the basis of capital.

What has to be done, however, is to follow through the further development of potential crisis—the real crisis can only be presented on the basis of the real movement of capitalist production, competition and credit—insofar as crisis arises from the forms characteristic of capital, its properties as capital, and not from its mere existence as commodity and money.[44]

If there is to be an explanation of crises in the Understanding, it is not to be found in the realm of circulation. Only the possibility is presented there. Marx indicates that the dialectical triad represented by the three books of *Capital* point to Volume III with its declining rate of profit and the overproduction of capital as well as its treatment of the credit system which contains the description of crisis. He says that the *immediate* statement of the value and wage theory of capitalism is in Volume I of *Capital*. It contains the need for a crisis but cannot show its workings until the immediate value relationships are *mediated* by Volume II, *The Circulation of Capital,* which shows the relationship of values *to each other as capital.* The exposition of the money nexus of capitalist production presents the formal possibility of crisis, that is, it negates Say's Law. By itself it cannot show how a crisis comes about. Volume II, he says, has to show the reproduction schema of capital circulation as they work, not as they break down. Therefore the solution to crisis is not to be found in circulation—underconsumption—as Marx himself pointed out to the Rodbertians. What is required is the synthesis of Volume III, *Capitalist Production as a Whole.* This work takes the necessity and the possibility of the first two volumes and combines them into the theory of declining rate of profit. It also provides a description of the credit system which Marx saw as a further cause of crisis.

Marx explains this in continuing on from the previous quotation:

The mere direct process of production cannot by itself add anything new in this connection. In order to exist at all, the conditions for it are assumed. For that reason, in the first section dealing with capital—the immediate process of production—no new element of crisis has to be added. *By its nature* crisis is present in it. For the process of production is appropriation and therefore production of surplus value. But this cannot appear in the process of production itself, because the latter is not concerned with the realization of both the reproduced value, and the surplus value. Crisis can only appear in the process of circulation which in essence is at the same time the process of reproduction. . . .

The circulation process as a whole or the whole process of reproduction of capital is the unity of its production phase with its circulation phases, a process which runs through both these processes as its phases. Therein lies a further developed possibility of abstract form of a crisis. The economists who deny crisis therefore insist only on the unity of these two phases. If they were only separate without being a unity, then no forcible restoration of their unity would be possible, no crisis. If they were a unity without being separate, then no forcible separation would be possible, which again is crisis. It is the forcible separation from each other of processes which in essence are one.[45]

I have concluded, however, that a decline in the rate of profit cannot be predicted with assurance and hence the theory is inadequate to support the hypothesis of increasingly severe depression. Then all we are left with is Marx's conviction that the contradictions in the wage bargain will resolve themselves through crisis. But, as argued in previous chapters, the contradiction is in the formulation of the wage bargain in value terms, not in the real nature of the bargain itself. In previous chapters, also, I have argued against this dialectical reasoning process in which the future is deduced from alleged contradictions in the present state without step-by-step explanation of the causes which lead from one situation to the next. It is evident then that Marx is blaming the observed crisis on the alleged contradiction, but he is not able to prove that the contradiction either exists **or** necessarily produces the crisis.

V · Revisionism and Proletarian Revolution: An Exercise in Applied Marxist Political Economy

A dualism runs through the whole monumental work of Marx . . . the work aims at being a scientific inquiry and also at proving a theory laid down long before its drafting. Marx had accepted the solution of the Utopians in essentials, but had recognised their means and proofs as inadequate. He therefore undertook a revision of them, and this with the zeal, the critical acuteness, and love of truth of a scientific genius. . . . But as Marx approaches a point when that final aim enters seriously into question, he becomes uncertain and unreliable. . . . It thus appears that this great scientific spirit was, in the end, a slave to a doctrine.[1]

Eduard Bernstein

"The final aim is nothing, the movement is everything"—this catchphrase of Bernstein's expresses the substance of revisionism better than many long arguments. The policy of revisionism consists in determining its conduct from case to case, in adapting itself to the events of the day and to the chops and changes of petty politics; it consists in forgetting the basic interests of the proletariat, the main features of the capitalistic system as a whole and of capitalist evolution as a whole, and in sacrificing these basic interests for the real or assumed advantages of the moment. . . . The ideological struggle waged by revolutionary Marxism against revisionism at the end of the nineteenth century is but the prelude to the great revolutionary battles of the proletariat which is marching forward to the complete victory of its cause despite all the waverings and weaknesses of the petty bourgeoisie.[2]

Lenin

The history of the years after Marx's death illustrates the consequences of basing a political program on a theory that is empirically meaningless. The years between 1890 and 1917 produced two absolutely contradictory policy proposals for scientific
socialism; both were consistent with the letter—although perhaps not the spirit—of Marx. The bitter battle between the
moderate revisionists and the militant Leninists over their opposing interpretations of Marx continues up to this day. In various ways and degrees it reveals the inability of Marx's theory to
give a clear course of action which is deducible from the doctrine
itself.

The late 1880s saw the end of a century of conversion of an
agrarian-mercantile economy in the Western world to an indus-
trial-capitalist society.[3] Marx's work had been drawn against the
backdrop of this process. To use Dobb's phrase, this was the
extensive expansion of capitalism; the size of the industrial reserve army was replenished by the drawing of new proletarians
into the factory system as the accumulation of capital pressed on
the old labor supply. At the same time agriculture itself was
being transformed from subsistence peasant agriculture to commercial capitalist farming. The net effect of these changes was
the shifting of labor from low productivity, noncapitalist agriculture, to more efficient types of production that resulted in
increasing amounts of relative surplus value being produced.

A nineteenth-century economist could not help but realize that
this extensive process must soon come to an end. Marx evidently
felt that increases in surplus value would henceforth have to
arise from accelerated absolute surplus value, that is, intensified
exploitation and lower real wage standard. The inability of the
rate of surplus value to rise sufficiently as a result of technological change in the industrial sector, would limit the effectiveness
of this counteracting cause to the decline in the rate of profit. In
turn the decline in the profit rate was but a harbinger of the
decline in the absolute amount of surplus value—the absolute
overproduction of capital. The end was in sight. Crisis and class

struggle were to intensify until the world revolution broke out.

Yet, instead of *la lutte finale* there was progress of the proletarian toward a higher standard of living and greater economic
bargaining power. The class struggle might have been intensified
in the sense that a series of intense strike actions took place; but
the significant fact was that these battles were marked, inter-
nationally, by important labor victories. These were the years in
which trade unions and the transactions of collective bargaining
became accepted as a normal part of the institutions of capitalism. One need only review the well-known history of the labor
movement in Britain, Germany, France, and the United States to
realize that while the trade unions may have come into existence
as a reaction to poor labor conditions, they did not remain pre-
cariously organized institutions which were perpetually at a
bargaining disadvantage with respect to the employers.

The process of redressing the balance of bargaining power between employers and labor was the substance of the intellectual
debate over ultimate solutions to the problems of wage labor.
The theorists argued the pro and con of socialism at all intellectual levels from Edward Bellamy's science fiction *Looking
Backward* to the sophisticated social commentary of the English
Fabians. For these people socialism was but the ultimate symbol
of a program of practical social reform which explored all ave-
nues of amelioration of the misery of the lower strata of the
working class. They were more akin to the thought that ranged
from Muckrakers to Margaret Sanger to Mary Baker Eddy, than
to Marx.

The important fact was not the socialist slogans of the organized labor movement nor the intellectual socialism of the social
worker, but rather that the practical efforts of labor and social
movements had less and less to do with any theory—Marxist or
otherwise. In the industrial nations the labor movement and its
sympathizers were finding pragmatic methods of sharing in the
gains of increasing productivity. In fact, during this era, the
growth of the organized labor power was associated with periods

of cyclic growth of capitalism rather than its decline. The increases in the productivity of labor as a result of enlarged use of (constant) capital permitted higher real wages if not a larger relative share in the national product. Marx's presentiment that it was possible that the use values of commodities purchasable with variable capital increased along with increased rates of surplus value actually took place. Capitalism it seemed was able to expand along the capital intensive margin as well as extensively and hence Marx's expectation of capitalism's imminent collapse was thus undermined. To the practicing labor leader this evaluation brought about a growing disparity between revolutionary socialist theory and the practice of "business unionism."

It was inevitable that someone from the Marxist camp would step forward with the demand that Marx's theory be revised in light of the success of the methods of labor practitioners like Sam Gompers. It was also natural that this person should be a German, since more than in any other country, German Marxists were deeply involved in the trade union leadership. Eduard Bernstein's *Evolutionary Socialism* was the long overdue challenge to the Marxist orthodoxy.[4] Publishing shortly after Engels' death, he argued that Marx had been unable to show that capitalism was bound to collapse in the foreseeable future. Consequently, the task of socialist labor leaders was to work for the immediate welfare of the workers within the confines of the wage system. Of course, the traditional Marxist believers in imminent revolution would also participate in such labor activity. But in practice their decisions on internal structure of labor organizations, their political activities, the requirements for party membership, the choice of bargaining and political weapons, the decisions on the profitability of compromises with opposing employers, the labor participation in "bourgeois" governments, all were contingent on whether the trade union program might be viewed as either an end in itself or a training ground for revolution. Bernstein's choice of the first of these two alternatives does, as Lenin charges, place him outside the Marxist revolutionary movement so far as practical action is concerned. It is true that, despite his protestations, Bernstein's program does not correspond to the revolutionary *intent* of Marx; but for us the point is not Bernstein's alleged opportunism but rather that Marx is shown to be unable to prove that revolution is an immediate necessity.

The impact of this conclusion on Social-Democratic parties was tremendous. Had the Bernstein critique come from without the socialist movement it would not have been as serious a challenge. A radical workingman could shrug off a pedantic Böhm-Bawerk as a "vulgar economist," but a life-long friend of Engels, and a labor leader in his own right, had to be reckoned with.

Despite important theoretical and expository weaknesses, Bernstein is effective in manipulating the nonfalsifiability of Marxism to push for his reformist program. As shown, the materialist concept of history has to contain within it its ideological opposite. Historical materialism is only stated as an *ultimate* truth, that is, in the long run the ideological must bow to the material. In effect Bernstein, having come under English empiricist influence through his contact with the Fabians, said, like Keynes, that in the "long run we are all dead." Within any finite time horizon it is impossible to determine a priori which of the contraries will predominate, the ideological factors or objective class interests based on material relations. It is ironic that by claiming to be a disciple of Marx, Bernstein is more damaging to revolution than Marx's enemies. He does not attempt to refute the irrefutable, but rather hoists Marx on his own petard. To be sure in the indefinite future capitalism will collapse. But Marx made the minor quantitative error of underestimating the strength of the counteracting ideological factors. At the present these factors are so powerful that to base labor strategy and tactics on the expectation of the imminent collapse of capitalism and the urgent necessity to prepare for revolution is to miss the current real "pork chop" issues. The result of an extremist program would be to alienate labor from Marxism. The interests of both labor and socialism are served by a revision of applied Marxism to correspond to the more moderate circumstances of the time.

In particular, Bernstein continues, Marx underestimated the growth of the democratic ethic. As mankind advances in productivity from the earliest subsistence stages of society to affluence its essence changes. Ideological factors become more significant and the time required for the materialist long-run effects to dominate becomes longer. To be sure, he says, democracy arose as the early battle cry of the bourgeoisie; but Marx mistakes origin for essence. Democracy is not a form of bourgeois class rule; it is an ideology "in principle the suppression of class government, though it is not yet the actual suppression of classes." [5]

The growth of the democratic tradition has made the state the vehicle for the collective bargaining of opposing classes rather than the instrumentality for the dictatorship of the bourgeoisie. In fact, the maintenance and development of the democratic state is in part contingent on the countervailing power of the trade unions. The interest of labor is in the preservation of democracy, the participation in its parliamentary councils, and the securing of the maximum political and economic power.

Bernstein argues that to follow what was to become the Leninist prescription—to break up the bourgeois state machinery— would be to take the very means of progress out of the hands of the labor movement. Precisely by using the democratic state and its institutional strength can labor achieve a deterrent to the counter attack of the employers to union advance.

Democracy, then, is a meaningful force outside of its class context. It shows viability in the face of attack and exerts a morally coercive discipline on members of all classes including the bourgeoisie itself. Conflicts of economic interest are real enough, but are, at least in principle, negotiable within the democratic political framework defined by Bernstein. The contrast between democracy and a dictatorial regime is that in the latter, violent revolution, as the only means of redress of grievance, is always present in incipient form. While

in a democracy the parties, and the classes standing behind them, soon learn to know the limits of their power. . . . Even if they make their demands rather higher than they seriously mean in order to give way in the unavoidable compromise—and democracy is the high school of compromise—they must still be moderate. The right to vote in a democracy makes its members virtually partners in the community, and this virtual partnership must in the end lead to real partnership.[6]

While this last sentence is, perhaps, somewhat too sanguine, Bernstein's account is close to the Western collective bargaining experience as variously expressed by its practitioners from Commons to Galbraith.

Accepting the democratic ethic himself, Bernstein presses on to argue that the question of a transformation of society to socialism must wait until the proletariat is in a majority, or at least until it can secure the voting support of the majority of the population. The working class cannot justifiably impose its will on the other members of society. The dictatorship of the proletariat is as immoral politically as is a dictatorship of the bourgeoisie.

Bernstein not only advances a normative objection to a minority revolution but says that the practical fact is that the proletariat is not ready for the seizure of power. Firstly, it is not homogeneous in its economic interest. Referring to the restrictive aspect of trade unionism (jurisdictional disputes, empire building, craft exclusiveness, and the like), he says that the labor movement does not have the unity necessary to rule without the individuals and groups involved falling out among themselves. Secondly, anticipating the argument advanced by Ludwig von Mises, he says the proletariat does not possess the economic sophistication to operate a planned economy.[7]

It is true that these practical objections seem to carry overtones of a radical overwhelmed by the prospect of actually having to

carry out the revolution he has been advocating. It may be that
Lenin's barb of "opportunism" may be an accurate description
of the source of Bernstein's anxiety. But individual psychology is
irrelevant. Bernstein's lack of militancy does not make his analysis wrong any more than Marx's humanitarian impulses make his
economics right. All these issues objectively turn on the question
of the likelihood of a *Zusammenbruch* of the capitalist system.
Bernstein conceded that such an eventuality would require the
abandonedment of reform and progress in favor of the violent
change which may perforce have to dispense with democratic
niceties. He held, however, the inevitability of such a collapse
was not demonstrated by Marxian breakdown arguments as they
were known in his day.

Rosa Luxemburg was already at this time advocating underconsumption as an explanation of depressions and imperialism. Along
with the orthodox Marxists, Bernstein rejected this thesis. He
was only a little less skeptical of the declining rate of profit
theory than of underconsumption. The tendency of the rate of
profit to decline could only be represented as a secular tendency
which might be effective in the long run. Further it was subject
to the counteracting causes which Bernstein was not sure would
fail to overcome the original tendency. Also, Bernstein was im-
pressed by the empirical content of the Austrian marginal utility
school. While he was willing to consider it only as an alternative
formulation to the labor theory of value, he was not willing to
base extremes in revolutionary policy on the declining rate of
profit prediction which was so closely dependent on the labor
theory. Indeed influenced by his British contacts he was really
unwilling to base a practical conclusion on any purely theoretical
argument.

The remaining possibilities were the ones generally accepted
by the orthodox Marxists of the time: (1) concentration of capital into monopolies and (2) the planless anarchy of capitalist
production might lead to crises of disproportionate production in
different sectors of the economy. Here Bernstein produced sta-

tistical argument that the average degree of monopoly was not proceeding as rapidly as anticipated by Marx. Even if monopoly were advancing in some industries, new industries were springing up in which the small entrepreneur was not yet obsolete. Thus while there were large aggregations of restrictive economic power they had not stifled growth in other noncompeting fields.

Somewhat inconsistently with the first argument, Bernstein argued that perhaps trusts and cartels were able to mitigate crises of disproportion. The anarchy of production was giving way to regulation and conscious planning by the trust.[8] More realistically Bernstein pointed to the growth of the credit system and the development of flexible money market institutions which make the second type of crises less likely.

It is not necessary for our purpose to show that Bernstein's economic propositions were right. Many economists would take issue with the propositions of the limited degree monopoly which has actually taken place, the degree and effectiveness of monopolistic planning, and the adequacy of flexible credit-money supply. The point is that his basic argument is not inconsistent with Marx's economic reasoning. As we have shown, following Joan Robinson, it may very well be, even within the bounds of Marx's system, that capitalism might lead to improved living standards for the workers. While it might not be through monopoly that crises may be controlled, we have shown that there is no a priori Marxian proof that they must become more severe. Indeed Bernstein's remarks about the flexible credit system are harbingers of the contracyclical policies which have filled the economic literature since Keynes. So far, at least, these have been effective in sparing us the wringer of general bankruptcy, although we still are burdened with the microeconomic problems of loss of efficiency due to price inflexibility underwritten by the guarantee of full employment.[9] At the same time, there is no guarantee of the increasing welfare possibility which we have suggested, any more than the increasing misery forecast can be made certain.

Now clearly Marx did not advocate reform. He expected that the sharpening of class conflict would lead to revolution. There is not the slightest difficulty in producing quotations from Marx and Engels in which the evolutionary view is denounced. The point is that to take the facts into account Marx had to include opposing contraries in his theory, and hence could not avoid at least the logical possibility of the counteracting causes dominating those of inevitable revolution.

Lenin took up the cause of attacking Revisionism from the faltering Kautsky. The main burden of his polemic was that Marx himself was not a moderate, and in quoting him he stresses the material thesis of the dialectical contradictions between material and ideological phases of social evolution. In contrast to Bernstein's ideology of democracy, Lenin asks what is the material *essence* of the state. With Marx and Engels he concludes that it is to be found in the class nature of society.[10] The state is testimony to the irreconcilability of class conflict; it is the forcible instrument of the ruling class for the perpetuation of its exploitation of labor, be it serf, slave, or proletarian. The particular form of state, then, is determined by productive relations through the class structure of the society from which it springs. It does not stand above material relations of production, but is shaped by them. Consequently there is a slaveowner state, a feudal state, a capitalist state—and a proletarian state, the dictatorship of the proletariat.

No reference to political institutions is meaningful to Lenin unless it is stated in terms of the universal categories of these historical class relations. Thus democratic political institutions are "the best possible shell for capitalism" since the property relations which imply exploitation are not dependent on the individual strengths and weaknesses of rulers. The element of forceful exploitation is not apparent, but the exploitative property relations of capitalism exist and are protected physically by the state and its police.[11] Democracy "is also a state. . . . Revolution alone can 'put an end' to the bourgeois state."[12] To consider democracy, as such, in political affairs is meaningless idealism to Lenin; the democratic state as a material force was brought into existence by the bourgeoisie in its struggles against the *ancien regime*. Marx, says Lenin, had held that the important question of democracy was that it is a bourgeois form of the state. The destiny of the proletariat was to revolt against the bourgeois ruling class and hence also its state; they must "break it up" and substitute the rule of the proletarian state. Frankly calling itself a class dictatorship, the proletarian state was to remain in existence until, with the utter defeat of the remnants of bourgeois influence, the need for any state as an oppressive force will end. The state will then "wither away."

There are two possible interpretations of the Marxian theory of the state: (1) The meaningful view can be identified as a *conspiracy theory*. Here the state machinery is a conspiracy of human flesh-and-blood bourgeoisie who buy and sell political figures and thus maintain class control. (2) The nonfalsifiable view is a dialectical deduction of the nature of the state from the existence of private property as an institution which excludes nonowners from disposition of material assets. Since the state in this last view is merely the protector of the property institution it does not require the conscious connivance of exploiters; we can refer to this as the *objective interpretation*.

Consider the conspiracy version. Few would argue that what we know as democratic government in the United States is a sham in which the political figures are conscious, cynical, paid agents of capitalists dedicated to perpetuating the exploitation of the working class. This is not to deny, unfortunately, that there are not a dearth of cases of political office being utilized for personal economic gain; but certainly the administration of, say, Franklin Roosevelt could not be characterized as a conspiracy of the bourgeoisie. It is doubtful that Roger Blough could have been called upon to testify that he had the Kennedy government in his pocket.

The Marxist retort is that in a country like the United States

the "best interests" of the capitalists is often served by the con-
cessions made by its more liberal wing. The decisions made by
this group occasionally entail the disciplining of recalcitrant individuals of their own class. Such a hedge can be used to explain
any action of the state within the conspiracy theory thus making
it meaningless. More significant, however, is that this argument
reveals the effective means whereby disputes between powerful
economic groups may be settled without, at least overt, resort to
violence. The democratic machinery is binding. That faction
which can secure the national electoral backing of all classes
prevails since the democratic ethic is more or less accepted by all
classes. Were the democratic machinery to be sufficiently flouted,
it is most probable that the majority would be able to provide
sufficient physical violence to restore it.

If this is the case, the next question is whether this machinery
of electoral power is available to the labor movement. Acquaint-
ance with contemporary politics in the West convinces the observer that the organized labor movement plays a large part in
the control of political power. Certainly labor governments are
in flat contradiction to the conspiracy thesis. All that could remain is the possibility that the entire leadership of labor governments is made up of the corrupt agents of employers who cyni-
cally receive their constituents with 100 percent success. One
reads language like this in the works of Lenin, but it is difficult
to believe that he would wholly depend on successful individual bribery for his case.

It seems more likely that, even though Lenin points to instances
of the conspiracy thesis, he is really arguing that whatever his
intentions *objectively* the moderate labor leader is committing
class treason. The willingness of a trade unionist to operate within
the confines of the wage system commits him to becoming an
agent of the capitalist class in practice. The bribery of which
Lenin speaks is that of the upper strata of the working class
which under conditions of imperialism can benefit from the overseas success of the capitalists and loses its will to revolution. If

Lenin is to take the facts of increased labor power and progress
into account in the industrially advanced nations he has to
abandon the meaningful conspiracy theory and retreat to the
objective version.

In the objective theory, the capitalist state is cast in the role
of the defender of the private property concept. *As such,* it is
the violent police agency for maintaining labor exploitation.
Trade union success does not falsify the thesis because trade
unionism operates on the premise of capitalist production. But,
says Lenin, let the workers once challenge the property funda-
mentals of the wage system—let their demands become confisca-
tory of capital—then the state shows its true nature by defend-
ing the ownership of private capital. The essence of the state is
the enforcement of property and contractual institutions by
various types of force.

Since this thesis is able to subsume in it the rise of the political power of organized labor, it loses its meaning under conditions of continued accumulation of capital and increasing real
labor income. It becomes operationally meaningful only under
circumstances where socialism is a practical question, that is,
the end of capitalist property institutions is immediately at stake.
In other words, if it cannot be shown that capitalism is about to
break down, the fact remains that access to democratic political
power is reasonably available to all classes. In ideological terms,
the theory of pragmatic efforts to improve working conditions
by means of bargaining and enlarging the democratic franchise
turn out to be more useful to labor than disquisitions on the
class essence of society and its state. If the counteracting causes
to increasing misery are operative—in part by the means of the
labor exercise of the franchise—then the state might indefinitely
reflect the economic interests of various classes within the collective bargaining type of transaction.

In contemporary Marxist literature the distinction between
these two versions of the theory of the state is blurred over with
serious programmatic results. The confusion is found in extreme

form in Paul Sweezy's *Theory of Capitalist Development*.[13] After presenting the Marxist transcription of the underconsumptionist aspect of Keynes, Sweezy examines the possibility of maintaining full employment by governmental countercyclical fiscal policy to raise consumption. Invoking the first version of the conspiracy thesis he argues that since the state is the instrument of the bourgeoisie it cannot be involved as a *deus ex machina* to serve the national economic interest at the cost of delaying the downward flexibility of wages during depressions. Rather than increase wages or supplement wages by transfer payments the bourgeois state will not operate in its own best interest by increasing final demand. We have already criticized Sweezy's version of the business cycle and his consequent countercyclical policy which is required to be mostly oriented to increasing consumption. It must be admitted that Sweezy is right in saying that hitherto massive government expenditures have had to be justified on the basis of military necessity. But the striking aspect of his analysis is the a priori conviction that the bourgeoisie will not help itself despite the advice of its *own* academic economists.

We conclude that the oppressive nature of the capitalist state, to Lenin, consists not so much in the mistreatment of the proletarian and the denial of his political franchise as in its resistance to the imminent, inevitable revolution. It follows from Lenin's view that the question of majority rule as a concept of democracy is secondary to the question of which class rules. Since it must be either the dictatorship of the bourgeoisie or that of the proletariat, it is both proper and necessary that even if it is a minority of the population, the proletariat should seize political power if a revolutionary conjuncture of events should present itself.

Thus Lenin's conclusions from the Marxian premises are the opposite of Bernstein's. The masses should be exposed to experiences which will demonstrate the impossibility of a compromise between classes. When the crisis of the inevitable revolutionary situation arises, that is, when neither the bourgeoisie or the proletariat can continue in the old manner, the proletariat will be trained and willing to seize power.[14] If this is properly accomplished the other classes—the peasantry, the petty bourgeoisie, the intellectuals—either will be neutralized or will follow the lead of the workers in at least tacit agreement. The democratic institutions, especially the unions, are not to be ignored, but they operate on the *premise* of capitalist class relations. Hence they are not revolutionary organizations, and their growth cannot be considered as an end in itself. They are to be pushed and prodded into increasingly militant positions so as to provide the "training grounds for revolution." Lenin considers the unions as spontaneous organizations of the workers who, unawakened by the Marxist ideology, could only conceive of bargaining within the framework of capitalism.[15] But as a result of the tactics pursued by the Leninists, they are to find themselves in the extremes of conflict with the capitalists. They will then draw the appropriate conclusions as to the essential class nature of the state and return to the scientific socialism proffered by the Marxist intellectual.

For Lenin, the working-class movement is not identical with unionism, but, transcending its collective bargaining organizational form, the workers must form a new (Soviet) type of revolutionary action organization. These direct action committees form the basis for the state machinery of the proletarian dictatorship.

Lenin, then, has drawn revolutionary tactical conclusions from the same Marxist premises which led Bernstein to humanitarian reformism. The tragicomedy of Marxist movements is the oscillation of party line between these two revolutionary and reformist approaches.

Prior to 1914, the increasing standard of living in the West, as the development of a high consumption economy proceeded, began to cast increasing doubt on the Leninist calculation. If revolutionary Marxism were to prevail over Revisionism, Lenin had to explain the fact of improved labor conditions and the apparent absence of the crisis of overproduction of capital in the mature capitalist nations. The militant now had to meet Bernstein's challenge and show *how* capitalism was breaking up. If Lenin pressed for revolution now, he could not postpone the issue of the breakdown to the distant future. Capitalism had to be shown to be presently in its tertiary stage, and the proletarian revolution was needed only to administer the *coup de grâce*.

Lenin's book *Imperialism, The Highest Stage of Capitalism* was an attempt to fill this need.[16] Imperialism is defined by Lenin in an unusual way. It is the monopoly stage of capitalism when "the fundamental attributes . . . of perfect capitalist competition are now . . . transformed into their opposites." [17] The apparently semantic issue of definition really involves the question of the inevitability of the expansionist economic and political national policy usually associated with the word. Lenin attempts to show that monopoly is the cause of these policies and therefore imperialism is not a matter of voluntary action by the bourgeoisie but the inevitable result of the economic history of concentration of capital.[18]

Lenin's work introduced no new empirical information, but rather draws on the research of Hobson and Hilferding. He attempts to place the monopoly development within the framework of historical materialism. Marx had argued in effect that the internal economies of large-scale production would lead to monopoly. This "concentration of capital" into larger productive units is apparently not conceived of as limited by diminishing returns to scarce entrepreneurial or other factors.[19] Further, concentration is accompanied by growing centralization of capital into multiplant operations and larger collusive combinations which do not reflect technological cost economies.[20]

Lenin cites the now familiar statistics of concentration of ownership. Following Rudolf Hilferding's *Das Finanzkapital* he argues that ownership of productive wealth is dominated by the corporate form; and, echoing the Veblenian critique, he points out that ownership in this form tends to transform the entrepreneurial function into mere financial control. Economic power is here vested in a parasitic *rentier* class of absentee owners. The investment banks are seen to play an increasingly important role in the centralization of capital by engineering these combinations.[21] Progressively, the distinction between the industrial and mercantile capitalist entrepreneur on one hand and the money-lending (bank) capitalist on the other breaks down. The result is the organization of national and international financial-capital industrial empires.

In commenting on the monopoly development, Sweezy argues that, to a degree, it has served to relieve the strains that Engels and Marx thought were building up to the final crisis of capitalism in the last century. The decline in the *average* rate of profit becomes less significant for the monopolistic firm. By the familiar armament of restrictive practices it can obtain higher profits at the expense of the less well-organized sectors of the economy. Agriculture would, of course, be the leading species of this group of exploited small-scale industries. Further, insofar as output restrictions resulted in higher rigid prices and if the bargaining power of monopoly enabled it to resist pressures for higher wages, the real wages of the workers would be lowered. The rate of surplus value would thus be raised counteracting the decline in the profit rate to a limited extent.[22]

Much more significant from Lenin's point of view was the new approach which finance capital was described as playing with respect to other nations. The old Ricardian version of commercial intercourse among nations was associated with exchange among equals to their mutual advantage. In contrast to Ricardo, however, Marx argued that a nation might import more value than it exported. In fact this was the characteristic of foreign trade which Marx had listed as one of the counteracting forces to the decline in the profit rate. This is not the permanent trade imbalance theory such as later advanced by Rosa Luxemburg; it involves the import of commodities from other nations which would require a greater labor expenditure if manufactured domestically.[23]

Ricardo said that

No extension of foreign trade will immediately increase the amount of value in a country, although it will very powerfully contribute to increase the mass of commodities, and therefore the sum of enjoyments. As the value of all foreign goods is measured by the quantity of the produce of our land and labour which is given in exchange for them, we should have no greater value if, by the discovery of new markets, we obtained double the quantity of foreign goods in exchange for a given quantity of ours.

Ignoring rent factors by assuming infinite elasticity of supply Ricardo is able to say that the total value is the labor actually expended. Cheaper foreign goods may bring about a shift downward of a horizontal supply curve for a given good. Whether more or less value (labor) would be expended in this *particular* industry depends on the elasticity of demand, but the national product including that of *imported goods* could not exceed the domestic labor expended. Ricardo had argued that it would be impossible for a country to import more *value* than it exported because the measure of the value of the imports was the domestic labor which goes into the exports required to obtain them.

Marx had insisted that the imports of commodities was like an invention that was not completely adopted. Let us adopt my suggestions about a unit elastic demand curve being implicit in the Marxian theory and consider a circumstance in which there was originally an infinitely elastic supply (particular expenses) curve $W_1 P$. Marx argued that the imports of commodities was like an invention that was not completely adopted so we have a new upward sloping particular expenses curve FP, with lower cost intramarginal firms or imports. Prices remain the same at P, but the labor expended falls from OW_1PL to $OFPL$. Were the *same quantity* of goods to be sold as formerly, OL, it would be accomplished with less labor $OFPL = OW_2ZL$ and the value per unit would be W_2. But were the goods to be sold at their value, more of them would be purchased $(OQ - OL)$, and the same sum of the prices OW_1PL would be still equal to the sum of their values OW_2HQ. (Notice I am not saying that they are *produced* along W_2HQ, since then the prices would be less than the values by $ZHLQ$. Value considered as a cost must be a hypothetical quantity of labor content per unit of product as if it were sold at the value, but produced according to an inelastic supply function.) Ricardo is right! With the *same* labor one either gets more products or allocates the saved labor in other directions if one chooses to have the old, smaller batch of products.

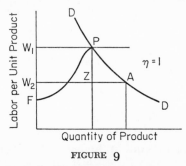

FIGURE 9

In any case, Marx says, the limited increase in value imported would not be sufficient to stem the tendency of the profit rate to fall. He further argues that eventually the extra capital accumulated would then press anew with greater force on the supply of labor power and accelerate the increase of organic composition of capital.

Both Ricardo and Marx agreed that foreign trade would tend to raise the rate of profit insofar as the increased sum of "enjoyments" amounted to cheaper subsistence of the proletarians and consequently a lower wage rate. Economies in the cost of constant capital might be achieved. Both elements would tend to retard the decline in the profit rate. Dominant nations might utilize the mercantilist bag of tricks to worsen the terms of trade of subject or colonial nations in order to raise their own individual rates of profit.

Lenin argued that the late nineteenth and twentieth centuries were characterized by a qualitatively different international relationship from that which Marx described. The essential new feature was the export of capital by advanced—monopolistic—

nations. He would not deny that the traditional forms of trade continued, but instead of buying commodities from colonies for resale to achieve a mercantile profit, capital appears now as a buyer of indigenous labor power for the production of surplus value. In addition to the sale of consumer commodities to the captive market of colonial areas at unfavorable terms of trade to buttress the rate of profit, exports shift to capital equipment to provide the means of production for the employment of native labor. Thus Lenin was able to account for the increase in the profit rate of the imperialist country without the balance-of-payments absurdities in which Rosa Luxemburg had become embroiled.

Bringing their monopolistic restrictionism with them, imperialist nations do not simply transport *laissez-faire* capitalist enterprise to less developed nations, but seek to restrict output as much as possible to limit it to noncompeting industries. The monopolist investor seeks a special advantage—a "concession." Imperialism, consequently, involves the division of the world among nations and financial oligarchies into monopolistic spheres of influence.

From this characterization of imperialism Lenin produces three lemmas:

(1) Imperialism tends toward the preservation of precapitalist productive relations in subject nations. Public utilities and transportation systems are developed only as they are complementary to the extractive and agricultural industries in which the backward economy has a "comparative advantage." These latter industries are operated on the basis of feudal and tribal social forms which are simply taken over by the imperialist nation. The local ruler becomes the overseer of the monopolist. The economy is kept unbalanced in favor of the extractive industries; there is little incentive on the part of imperialism to organize factory production, develop skilled native labor forces, and stimulate entrepreneurship. Not only does imperialism perpetuate the technical backwardness of older societies, it also destroys their social

structure in exposing them to the corrosive effects of the market. The ethic of mutual assistance and the security of a static social structure of rights and duties characteristic of precapitalist civilizations vanishes. It is not compensated for by greater material welfare based on higher levels of productivity as is characteristic of advanced nations.

One main "contradiction" of imperialism is the conflict between the monopolistic interest of the dominant nation and the retarded but inevitable growth of a native bourgeoisie. These colonial entrepreneurs chafe at the restrictions imposed on them. A virulent nationalism inevitably springs from their lack of social status, the impoverished domestic market for their products, the uneducated and undernourished labor supply, and the support of obsolete feudal institutions, as well as the direct disabilities imposed by the mother country on their field of economic operations. Despite their own mutual class antagonism those nationalist movements involve native proletarians as well as their own employers.

(2) The export of capital relieves the pressure of accumulation on the rate of profit. Instead of bidding for the scarce labor factor and increasing its organic composition, capital flows overseas to areas of cheap labor supply and into investments in the agricultural and extractive industries with low organic composition. Capital thus raises its average rate of profit and maintains or increases the rate of exploitation at home. This is the main counteracting cause to which Lenin ascribes the new lease on life acquired by capitalism after Marx's death.[24]

Taken at face value this seems absurd, since if no net value may be imported, *mutatis mutandis,* value may not be exported either. Balance of payments considerations require that an equivalent value be imported from colonial countries. If, however, it is seen that imports from colonial countries include the purchase of colonial assets—labor power and means of production—the balance of payments requires that the export of capital really means the following equation:

Merchandise exported from the metropolis plus repatriated profit = assets held abroad in labor power and means of production plus exports of consumer goods and means of production to the metropolis.

From the point of view of goods delivered to and taken from the metropolis it appears as if more merchandise is exported than imported, just as Rosa Luxemburg suggested (modified to account for repatriated earnings on assets held abroad). Further if the value exported exceeds the value of goods physically transferred to the metropolis, if the variable capital proportion of both the exported merchandise and the imported merchandise are the same were they both manufactured in the mother country, the effect is that a greater value is produced with smaller variable capital by the metropolis labor. In this sense the rate of profit is enlarged by increasing the rate of surplus value. Similarly the organic composition might be decreased by the import of cheap raw materials. It is misleading, however to suggest that the export of capital consists of the transfer of value as opposed to an export surplus on current account, that is, a "sink for savings" when in fact they mean the same thing.

However interpreted, such capital export raises the rate of profit. Now not only is capital able to expand extensively once more, but some of the extra profit derived from colonial empire is shared with influential segments of the proletariat of the metropolis. Monopoly is able to distort the wage structure in favor of the articulate skilled workers. They become corrupt, lose their revolutionary vigor, and, Lenin contends, become the "palace slaves" of the employers.

The favored economic status of the "aristocracy of the working class" gives rise to the class treason of Revisionism. Trade union leadership drawn from this group deserts to the employers on crucial issues at the expense of the interests of the mass of the less fortunate proletarians. The rate of exploitation is maintained or increased. But even this last effect may be modified if account is taken of the value terms in which Marxists describe exploitation. If imperialism is associated with more favorable terms of trade with colonial areas resulting from neomercantilist practices or the employment of cheap native labor, the importation of cheaper articles consumed by proletarians may result in a rise in domestic real wages in use-value terms.[25] The analysis is the same as the possibility of sharing the increases in productivity due to technological innovation between the workers and the employers even though innovation appears in Marxian terms as increases in the production of relative surplus value and heightening of the rate of exploitation.[26] Insofar as this improved status of the entire working class of the advanced nation results from the degradation of colonial labor rather than from a technological advantage in colonial production of some commodities, the entire class may be said to have been corrupted by imperialism. This aspect is not emphasized by Lenin who wishes to reserve his fire for the Revisionist trade union leaders and to win over the rank and file.

Nevertheless, despite all the restrictions, Lenin argues that in the long run, capitalism will spread to the colonial nations. The inevitable forward march of society accelerated by contact with developed nations will not be denied. The resultant nationalism will oust foreign rule and end the flow of superprofit which might be shared with the aristocracy of the working class. In the ultimate, the interest of the proletarians of the ruling country is to make common cause with those of colonial nations. Lenin makes this internationalism the crucial test of proletarian morality.

(3) The division of the world into monopolistic spheres of influence results in an uneasy international balance of power. Lenin assumes that military power is derivative of economic power. It is on the basis of economic productive capacity that the equilibrium is maintained. Since the balance is disturbed by differential rates of economic development, interimperialist wars must inevitably break out. Lenin asks, "Is there *under capitalism* any means of remedying the disparity between the development of

productive forces on the one side, and the division of colonial 'spheres of influence' by finance capital on the other—other than by resorting to war?" [27]

Lenin's epigram is that "imperialism is capitalism in its moribund stage." It brings on itself the revolutionary force of the entire colonial world of all classes. The temporary melioration of the inherent class conflicts within the metropolis which imperialism engendered finally comes to an end. Fratricidal warfare breaks out among the capitalists. The final crisis of capitalism can break out in any combination of these forms—as well as the cyclical downturn—and precipitate a revolutionary situation. Lenin concludes that the most dangerous opponents of the proletarian revolution are not the bourgeoisie themselves, whose antagonism to socialism is taken for granted, but the reformists. Lenin reserves his special fire for the Revisionists who are accused of making a token genuflection to Marx, but who delude workers into temporarily sharing in monopolistic profits at the expense of their long-term interests.

The most striking aspect of Lenin's argument is that the facts adduced are not Marxist discoveries. The denunciation of monopoly and imperialism was a familiar aspect of American populist-agrarian-labor social criticism which ranged in sophistication from William Jennings Bryan to Thorstein Veblen. Lenin's addition was to hitch these observations onto the Marxist doctrine of the inevitability of the collapse of capitalism and the class nature of the state. Insofar as Lenin repeated the observation and charges of these Western forerunners, he was demonstrating what W. W. Rostow's "Non-Communist Manifesto" calls the "Marxist half- or quarter-truth." [28] Certainly the egocentric profit maximization motive led to the colonialization of the dark-skinned majority of mankind. But Rostow goes on to argue that the revolution which unleashed the profit motives in the eighteenth century also contained "within its presuppositions the case for free elections . . . for destroying or controlling monopolies; for social legislation which would set considerations of human welfare off against profit incentives; and above all, for the progressive income tax." [29]

For Lenin it is inconceivable that the trust could be regulated in the public interest by the state. And yet it is a hard truth that no matter how halting and unsatisfactory, or inadequately staffed, particular aspects of antitrust law enforcement may be, a significant limitation of monopoly is an evident fact of our economic life.[30] To be sure this has not been a result of the altruism of the monopolistic firms. But the striking fact is that even though control may have arisen from agrarian and labor pressures it has not resulted in either the demise of capitalism or the violent reaction of the bourgeoisie.

The essential question raised by Lenin's *Imperialism* is whether opposition to imperialism necessarily implies opposition to capitalism itself. Does the capitalist system stake its survival on the colonial system and spheres of influence and the exploitation of smaller nonmonopolist capitalists? Can accumulation continue without it? We are brought back, once more, to the theory of crises and Bernstein's critique of the breakdown theory. If one rejects the imminent breakdown theory then imperialism is not a necessary capitalist policy for its survival. There is then no absolute *obstacle* to the nonrevolutionary reformist solution to the issues of colonialism, prevention of imperialist wars, and improvement of labor standards.

Lenin assumes that this is impossible on the most doctrinaire grounds:

It goes without saying that if capitalism could develop agriculture . . . if it could raise the standard of living of the masses, who are everywhere still poverty-striken and underfed, in spite of the amazing advance in technical knowledge, there could be no talk of a superfluity of capital. . . . But if capitalism did these things it would not be capitalism; for uneven development and wretched conditions are premises of this mode of production. . . .

Assuming the impotence of the labor movement he goes on:

As long as capitalism remains what it is, surplus capital will never be utilized for the purpose of raising the standard of living of the masses in a given country, for this would mean a decline in profits for the capitalists; it will be used . . . by exporting capital abroad to the backward countries. . . . The necessity of exporting capital arises from the fact that in a few countries capitalism has become "overripe." . . . and cannot find "profitable" investment.[31]

It is true that while Lenin's view is hopelessly rigid, it is not automatically to be considered a false characterization of some of the evils of monopoly and economic nationalism. Rostow makes the very apt comment that the Western nations pushed the world to the very brink of proving the Marxists right. Thus while contingent events do not prove historical necessity, the First World War and the ensuing Versailles Treaty seemed to make a mockery of any but the Marxist interpretation. Bernstein's abandonment of the general strike against war in 1914 and his shocking support of German colonialism (along with the Fabian endorsement of the Boer War and the First World War) seemed to verify Lenin's characterization of Revisionism as an opportunist movement.[32]

What would be overlooked in the acceptance of the Leninist description of these events was the evolution of criticism of imperialist policies by the non-Marxist left. It cannot be denied that the reformist social critics failed to carry the day. But the democratic ideology after the First World War was still represented by such people as Charles Beard, Clarence Darrow, Robert La-Follette, and Fiorello LaGuardia for the liberal Republicans and Woodrow Wilson and his young men among the liberal Democrats. Despite the crushing of the extreme left and the lack of development of the A. F. of L., it was not a foregone conclusion that short-sighted monopolistic self-interest must be equated with governmental policy.

The very accession to power by these elements under the Roosevelt Administration would have been a refutation of Lenin's thesis were it not for the circumstance that it occurred against the background of the Great Depression. It appeared that Lenin's theory of the inability of capitalism to operate on a self-sustained basis was verified. Capitalism, wrote Stalin, was in a period of general crisis in which escape from one disaster (for example, imperialist war) only meant the precipitation of another (crisis and stagnation).[33]

These two aspects of the Depression illustrate the distinction between verification and falsification which Popper has explained. *Any* crisis of capitalism might be construed as a verification of Lenin's thesis that the "bourgeois-democratic" state has not been able to mitigate depressions by measures which may raise consumption and wages or by regulating and disciplining monopolies. The state as the agent of the bourgeoisie is incapable of adopting measures which differ from any but the most immediate short-run class interest of the employers. But single empirical observations cannot provide universal necessity by verification of hypotheses; they can only falsify propositions. What observation would constitute a falsification of the Leninist idea? Obviously any stable nonimperialist government would qualify if it were willing to adopt some of these measures.

In the United States at least the New Deal patently would seem to qualify. It legislated in favor of greater power for labor and the relative restriction of monopolistic practices by capital. The sharing of state power was complemented by the Keynesian prescription for an economic policy which emphasized the mutual interest of labor and capital in high levels of national income. The enlightened self-interest of both classes in a high consumption economy has come to turn progressively less on the division of national income as on its enlargement. Galbraith and others have argued that in the absence of increasing misery the division of income can be tolerably relegated to the collective bargaining process even though it may be associated with the diseconomies of less-than-perfect competition.

Of course it was possible for Marxists to rationalize away the

New Deal as the tactical retreat of a beleaguered bourgeoisie threatened by the increasingly militant working class. But the rationalization does not account for the labor participation in political power; nor does it explain the support to labor on humanitarian or public interest grounds by political leaders who could not reasonably be characterized as subtle capitalist conspirators. In effect these years showed that given a program for the recovery from the Depression Bernstein's concept of democracy was indeed a workable one, even though his own underlying macroeconomics was Marxist instead of Keynesian.

If the Depression gave birth to a feasible reformist program of contracyclical domestic policy, the Second World War brought with it the end of colonialism. To be sure important formal and economic divisions of spheres of influence remain as well as remnants of colonial empire. The handwriting, however, is clearly on the wall. An outstanding aspect of this development is that it is not in contradiction to the continuation of capitalism. Precisely those powers that have divested themselves of overseas empire are the nations which have achieved the most rapid rate of growth. In Table 1 the mature Western nations are ranked by their growth in manufacturing in the last decade, since the Gross National Product is affected by the relative decline in the agricultural sectors and hence does not fully reflect the pace of economic advance or the ability to compete in world markets.

Of the seven nations with manufacturing growth rates in excess of 6 percent per annum, all but the minor exceptions of Austria and Finland had cut ties with overseas empire during this period of time. Of course the other classification of these nations (except Japan) as part of the expanding economy of Western Europe makes it impossible to show a simple causal connection between the end of empire and economic growth. In the case of France the abandonment of the *sale guerre* for the retention of empire against colonial nationalist revolutions has also been the solution of inflation and balance of payments problems induced by military expenditures. Here one might easily

Table 1

Annual Rate of Growth of Manufacturing Sector and Gross
Domestic Product in Mature Western Economies 1950–1960
(Percentage)

	Manufacturing	Gross Domestic Product
Japan	18.1	9.5
Germany (Federal Republic)	10.1	7.6
Italy	9.0	5.9
Austria	7.1	5.9
France	6.5	4.3
Netherlands	6.1	4.7
Finland	6.0	4.6
Australia	5.7	3.9
Norway	5.1	3.5
New Zealand	4.6	3.5
Belgium	4.1	2.9
United States	3.6	3.3
United Kingdom	3.5	2.7
Canada	3.4	3.8
Denmark	3.3	3.4
Sweden	3.3	3.2

Source: Adapted from *World Economic Survey 1961* (New York, United
Nations, 1961), p. 63.

argue for a direct salutary effect (on domestic investment and
economic growth) resulting from the end of colonialism.

Perhaps in Britain a positive effect on growth may yet be
achieved if investment and entrepreneurship are redirected from
their former export outlet to renewing the existing domestic industrial plant.[34] It is interesting to speculate on the degree to
which the entrepreneurship that had made Britain the "work-
ship of the world" had been transformed into a *rentier* mentality
by the colonial administrator role which she assumed by the end
of the nineteenth century.

It is also possible that the high *marginal* productivity of capital invested in colonial underdeveloped areas of relative capital

shortage resulted in investments where the *average* productivity
was considerably below that of Britain. Thus from the point of
view of the empire the total (average) productivity was most
increased by such an allocation; but from the point of view of
the industrial complex of the British Isles, capital may be
diverted away from maintaining its capacity to compete with
Germany and the United States in the sale of highly manufactured products. This view must be further qualified since much
of the capital invested in the empire may have been allocated
to administrative, military, transportation, sanitation systems.
These might not even have raised the internal productivity of
the colonial areas net of the cost to colonials; but their productivity to the mother country lay in the maintenance of conditions
under which colonial agricultural and labor-consuming manufactures could be placed on the world market. Here the marginal
productivity of investment overseas resulted less from a capital
shortage as such as from the peculiar circumstances of (1) the
comparative advantage of colonial areas in producing some
(tropical) commodities and (2) the fact that the precapitalist
institutions had to be revamped by the colonial powers before
these advantages could be realized on the world market.[35]

Finally, the downward pressure on money wages relative to
other costs resulting from the cheaper imported articles of consumption may have retarded the development of labor-saving
technology as well as the complementary labor skills which accompanied the high wage economy of the United States.

I have only suggested the *possibility* that colonialism was a
positive brake on economic growth. By cursorily examining the
issue from the point of view of the supply of factors of production, we leave open the question Lenin raised of its role in providing the investment demand which otherwise might have been
inadequate to maintain full employment of these factors. But it
is not necessary for us to provide the direct causal link here. The
point at issue is that the end of colonial empires and imperialist
foreign economic policy is not incompatible with increased eco-

nomic activity as Lenin had imagined. Regardless of whether there would have been sufficient investment opportunities without colonies in the nineteenth century, my analysis of the Marxian theory of the decline in the profit rates and the evidence of post-war history does not show that future private investment will necessarily be inadequate.

Lenin had hinted that the process of export of capital would transform Europe into a region of parasitic *rentiers* and their retinue largely devoted to exploiting foreign surplus value and producing services rather than basic industrial products. With the possible exception of Britain, this had not happened; but rather having disposed of colonial liabilities these nations have shown the possibility of self-sustaining noncolonial expansion at high rates of growth. Further, in the main the process of divestiture of colonial empire was accomplished peacefully—albeit reluctantly—without the last-ditch war of reaction associated with the death of an *ancien regime*. What Marxist of the prewar epoch would have conceived of the end of British rule in India without years of revolution? It emerges that imperialism cannot be shown to be capitalism in its moribund stage.

Once having achieved independence the former colonies have reacted contrary to a Leninist expectation and have in many cases been attempting to attract foreign capital to accelerate their rates of growth. "Many countries," comments the U.S. Department of Commerce,

have adopted measures in recent years which encourage, and in some cases make almost mandatory from a marketing standpoint, the extension of operations in those countries through the inflow of foreign capital. Many have enacted legislation intended to liberalize the treatment of private foreign investments and provide the necessary stability and security.[36]

In the three decades from 1929 through 1959 direct private investments by the U.S. in other nations has increased fourfold; of this, manufacturing increased 5.4 times. Contrary to Lenin's expectation, the relative growth of investment in manufacturing

Table 2

Private U.S. Foreign Direct Investments 1929–1959
(Billions of Dollars at Book Value and Percents of Total)

Industry	1929 Amount	%	1946 Amount	%	1950 Amount	%	1957 Amount	%	1959 Amount	%
Manufacturing	1.8	24	2.4	33	3.8	32	8.0	32	9.7	33
Petroleum	1.1	15	1.4	19	3.4	29	9.0	36	10.4	35
Mining and Smelting	1.2	16	.8	11	1.1	9	2.4	10	2.9	10
Public Utilities	1.6	21	1.3	18	1.4	12	2.1	8	2.4	8
Other Industries	1.8	24	1.3	18	2.1	18	3.7	14	4.3	14
Total	7.5	100	7.2	100	11.8	100	25.2	100	29.7	100

Source: Adapted from Pizer and Cutler, *U.S. Business Investments in Foreign Countries*, p. 1.

in such industries as chemicals, automobiles and transportation equipment, nonelectrical machinery, and primary and fabricated metals shows the tendency to stimulate the development of domestic industry in the country to which the capital is exported.[37] Marked declines are noted in the relative importance of the traditional colonial industries mining and smelting, public utilities, and "other" industries (including agriculture and trade). The full importance of the growth of manufacturing tends to be obscured by the use of the book value of assets as a measure of overseas operations by U.S. firms. The large fixed asset proportion of reserves and exploration cost in petroleum acquisitions would tend to overestimate the importance of petroleum in this dimension rather than in, say, employment or purchases from local firms.[38] Further, the petroleum assets tend to be concentrated in a few areas, for example, Venezuela and the Middle East, and therefore the totals do not reflect world-wide operations.

Since much of the manufacturing investment is concentrated in Western Europe, it is well to examine the distribution of investment by area in order to observe the changes in the less developed areas of the world. In Table 3 the percentages of manufacturing to total direct investment are calculated for each area.

Percentages of manufacturing to investments less petroleum are also calculated. Apart from other considerations this ratio is more consistent with the definitions used by the authors of the Department of Commerce study; they grouped all petroleum activities into a single industry group and in order to do so eliminated the refining operations from the manufacturing group where it is placed by the Standard Industrial Classification.[39]

While investment in Europe has concentrated in manufacturing reflecting the economic development of the area, it is the *change* in the composition of the investment in Latin America and the other less industrialized areas which has to be noted. In the thirty years under review the percentage of direct manufacturing investment in Latin America has doubled with respect to

Table 3

Foreign Private Manufacturing Component of U.S.
Direct Investment by Regions 1929–1959

	1929	1936	1943	1950	1957	1959
Canada						
Amount*	891	799	941	1897	3924	4558
Percent of Total Investment	41	41	40	53	45	45
Percent of Total less petroleum	42	43	42	60	59	59
Latin America						
Amount*	231	192	325	781	1280	1426
Percent of Total Investment	7	7	12	17	16	16
Percent of Total less petroleum	8	8	15	24	25	26
Europe						
Amount*	629	612	879	932	2195	2927
Percent of Total Investment	46	49	42	54	53	55
Percent of Total less petroleum	56	62	52	71**	76**	76**
Africa						
Amount*	7	10	13	55	106	120
Percent of Total Investment	7	11	10	19	16	14
Percent of Total less petroleum	10	19	15	34	27	24
Asia						
Amount*	76	54	68	60	190	248
Percent of Total Investment	19	13	18	6	9	11
Percent of Total less petroleum	27	21	29	26	42	43
Oceania						
Amount*	50	42	50	107	314	412
Percent of Total Investment	34	38	39	42	45	47
Percent of Total less petroleum	63	62	62	73	79	79

* In millions of dollars.
** The base of this percentage is diminished by large U.S. investment in the refining distribution of petroleum products in Europe, especially Britain.
Source: Adapted from *U.S. Business Investments in Foreign Countries,* pp. 93, 106.

total direct investment and more than tripled if the influence of the oil is eliminated. The increase in the amount of investment in manufacturing reflects the greater U.S. activity in capital export as well as the shift toward manufacturing.

The effect of operations by U.S. investors on the development of manufacturing can be observed by comparing the portion of direct U.S. investments devoted to manufactures as compared to percentage of manufacturing in the gross domestic product of the capital importing nation. As a marginal contribution to the total product, imported capital tends to raise the manufacturing component whenever it exceeds the percentage of domestic manufactures.

With the exception of Panama, Chile (see Table 4 note), and Peru, the effect of U.S. investments has been to increase manufacturing operations. Actually the proportions cited tend to underestimate this effect since petroleum refining which is such an important manufacturing process is included in the "Manufacturing Sector of Gross Domestic Product" in most analyses tending to enlarge it, compared to the U.S. Department of Commerce exclusion of petroleum refining from the category of manufacturing in the survey cited.[40]

Perhaps the most eloquent testimony to U.S. activity in industrial development is the preoccupation of academic "bourgeois economists" with this problem and the accession of many of them to high posts in governmental planning.

Of course, it is true that part of the motivation for this sort of program has been inspired by fear of the Soviet alternative. One reads, for instance, the comment of the Committee for Economic Development (CED) in urging further encouragement to investment in Latin America:

the efforts of leaders in underdeveloped countries to bring about economic progress can take the way of peaceful development and growing freedom, or can lead, through frustration, to violence, communist subversion or other forms of regimentation. . . . The Cuban revolution has brought these facts closer to home. . . . Such a revolution is certain to have the economic and political support of the Communist Bloc and to be a channel through which communist influence can be exerted in neighboring underdeveloped countries.[41]

The $1,096 million of net earnings after taxes on direct investments in Latin America in 1957 prompts the CED to the following comment on the size of U.S. investments in that area:

Table 4

Manufactures as a Percentage of Gross Domestic Product and Direct U.S. Investment in Manufactures in Selected Countries

	U.S. Direct Investment (1957–1959) in Foreign Nations[a]			Manufacturing Sector of Gross Domestic Product 1950–1959[b] (Percentage)
	Average Annual Total (Millions of Dollars)	Manufacturing as Percent of Total Investment	Manufacturing as Percent of Total Investment Less Petroleum	
Canada	9,382	45	59	27
Mexico	748	46	48	21
Panama	266	2	2	11
Argentina	341	46	*	22
Brazil	823	49	56	24
Chile	694**	3	*	18
Colombia	393	17	43	16
Peru	406	7	9	16
Venezuela	2,644	5	25	10
India	123	30	*	17
Japan	192	33	*	26
Philippines	344	22	*	13
Australia	659	53	*	27
New Zealand	51	32	*	21

* Petroleum operations are included in the total and are not distinguishable from it in the data.
** In Chile 96 percent of the investments were in mining and smelting, including the refinery operations which the S.I.C. includes in manufacturing in its analysis.

Sources: a. Adapted from *U.S. Business Investment in Foreign Countries*, pp. 89–90. b. *World Economic Survey, 1961* (United Nations), pp. 18, 61.

We do not . . . claim a philanthropic motive for United States business. . . . Businesses have gone to Latin America in the hope of making money, and on the whole they have made money. At the same time the activities of the United States business in Latin America have been extremely helpful to the host countries. The process is mutually beneficial, and would not be carried on unless this were so.[42]

It may very well be that Lenin's challenge to imperialism may have had the same gadfly effect in ending colonialism that Marx's did a century ago for the condition of the working class in Western Europe. The point is that steps can be taken to remedy real social evils. This is not to imply that the remedies are easy or without cost, but rather that we are dealing within the sphere of conscious social policy rather than the blind contradictions inherent in the inevitable march of history.

Viewed in perspective, Lenin's theory of imperialism implied a recognition that the center of revolutionary activity was shifting from the industrial west to the colonial world.[43] Stalin explained the Bolshevik revolution occurring in Tsarist Russia rather than in the advanced industrial West in terms of Lenin's theory of the imperialist stage of capitalism as "capitalism breaking at its weakest link." Nevertheless Lenin's remarks about deindustrialization of the West and its transformation into a latter-day tribute state suggest that he was aware of the growing unlikelihood of revolution in developed capitalist countries and was seeking a rationalization within Marxist theory. Thus in strategy and practice Lenin admitted the effectiveness of Bernstein's collective bargaining *modus vivendi* in advanced democratic nations, but thought that these nations would permanently prevent the development of the others. Thus Marxist militancy has become more and more the ideology of the radical wing of the underdeveloped nations which are attempting to achieve their capitalist "bourgeois-democratic revolution."

VI · Conclusions

I thought, that while the higher and richer classes held the power of government, the instruction and improvement of the mass of the people were contrary to the self-interest of those classes, because tending to render the people more powerful for throwing off the yoke: but if the democracy obtained a large, and perhaps the principal, share in the governing power, it would become the interest of the opulent classes to promote their education, in order to ward off really mischievous errors, and especially which would lead to unjust violations of property. On these grounds I was not only as ardent as ever for democratic institutions, but earnestly hoped that Owenite, St. Simonian, and all other anti-property doctrines might spread widely among the poorer classes; not that I thought these doctrines true, or desired that they should be acted on, but in order that the higher classes might be made to see that they had more to fear from the poor when uneducated, than when educated. . . .

Comte's work recognises no religion except that of Humanity, yet it leaves an irresistible conviction that any moral beliefs concurred in by the community generally, may be brought to bear upon the whole conduct and lives of its individual members, with an energy and potency truly alarming to think of. The book stands a monumental warning to thinkers on society and politics, of what happens when once men lose sight in their speculations, of the value of Liberty and Individuality.

John Stuart Mill [1]

Perhaps the most meaningful tribute to Marx is the fact that a book such as this is still justifiable and a new look at his work useful. There are only a few individual works which are close to a century old and yet must be criticized at their face value rather than from the more patronizing viewpoint of the history of economic doctrine. That Marx's system requires a serious rebuttal, even after one hundred years of refinement of the competing techniques of economic theory, is more significant than any faint praise.

It is no less true, however, that the main conclusion I have reached is that the basic source of Marx's errors was his typically nineteenth-century belief that evolutionary science would replace the *deus ex machina* of Cartesian determinism. The belief in the inexorable progress of a single universal essence toward its ultimate destiny, be it perfection or destruction, is everywhere evident in the ideology of the time.[2] We see it in the last century's view of biological evolution, the cyclical symphonic form or the music drama "ring," the romantic novel, social Darwinism, and the idyllic world of J. B. Clark.

The Hegelian description of this historical evolutionary spiral gained a wide influence even in England. A person like Alfred Marshall, thoroughly trained in empiricism and formal mathematical deduction, presented himself as a disciple of Spencer and "of history and philosophy, as represented by Hegel's *Philosophy of History* . . ."[3]

The extension of the doctrine of essence to the existence of an entity, the definition of which implies all its characteristics, is abetted by the hypostatization of abstract concepts into capitalized nouns characteristic of the German language. This Aristotelian thinking was, of course, not peculiar to the German philosophy, but it seems to have reached its highest development in that nation. Thus the relative statement of exchange values in the English Ricardian form, becomes a social crystal in Marx.[4] The struggle over value is the subject of class conflict and the ultimate cause of the inevitable breakdown of capitalism. Smith and Ricardo were certainly aware of conflicts of interest between capital and labor. But for Marx conflicts became Contradiction. Empiricism became a rationalist type of materialism. Pragmatic reform became revolution.

I have argued that for Marx the labor theory of value is a necessary extension of the materialist theory of history. It has been my contention that to make an evolutionary theory meaningful it must be stated so that the causal mechanics of each successive step in the evolution must be explained or a procedure specified for making the proper analysis. Marx attempted to provide such a demonstration for the demise of capitalism, although he did not feel that it was a prerequisite to adopting his revolutionary theory of history. In doing this Marx introduced another, equally metaphysical concept, value. Here the prediction of the inevitable breakdown of capitalism depends on the rigid limitation of national income by the labor value expended. We have followed the consequences of this concept and have seen how the Marxian analysis of wages and crises is its manifestations.

The abandonment of the rationalist approach brings us to the less comforting, but more specific, twentieth-century method. This revival of empiricism permits one to make probability statements about the consequences of economic activities if individuals behave as we observe them to or as we speculate they might in the future. This probabilistic form of our scientific statements has apparently carried the day in the physical as well as social sciences. It would be absurd, however, to dismiss the scientific advance of the last century because later work has required a different methodology. It is required, however, that earlier conclusions must not be treated as dogma but must be restated and qualified in terms of later research.

In important respects this need for critical review applies to the works of Marx. Marx more than anyone else would have demanded that his own work can be most legitimately evaluated as the product of his intellectual and material environment. Only the most obtuse reader can fail to realize that a century ago Marx raised the key economic questions of our time. He analyzed the problem of maintaining full employment through avoidance of underconsumption while avoiding a rate of expansion which brings about rising costs and declining investment. But, as we have seen, Marx's method of presenting this problem in absolute value terms makes its solution appear impossible. While denying Marx's thesis, it would be equally improper to argue that the economic problems of capitalism will be solved automatically. It might very well be that in any given institutional environment capitalism might not be politically able to make the adjustments in public policy. Current history has suggested to us that depending on the politics of each nation and its own economic peculiarities there will be a spectrum of degrees of social control of the economy rather than a monistic socialist solution. There is, however, no logically certain prediction possible about the future course of society. The point made in this essay is that the contingent facts of any one period of time must be considered before the next stage can be predicted or alterations in the institutional structure advocated. The belief that transcendental predictions were possible and indeed necessary for the scientific method led to the fatal rigidity in the Marxian system.

If one is able to overlook the rationalism in Marx, the true value of his perceptions becomes available to the economist. Marx stressed the significance of total economic activity as well as narrow pecuniary interest in determining individual social behavior. In this Marx was a pioneer of the new realism which marked social thinking in the latter part of the last century. While he was not the first to do so, Marx forcefully drew attention to the "decennial cycle," although he failed to explain sufficiently its critical points and to show that the trend is toward cycles of greater amplitude. In doing so he did preview the credit effects, the influence of bull-market psychology on speculation and investment, and the significance of the liquidity trap in discussing the hoarding of money. In his analysis of the cumulative contraction through reduced consumption Marx anticipated the multiplier analysis. In his denunciation of Say's Law of Markets, Marx spoke from the "underworld" seventy years before Keynes. He showed the possibility of sale without purchase. Finally, among what Samuelson calls Marx's "golden insights," we would have to list the reproduction schema which

show the aggregate flow of income among the various sectors of
the economy. Of course this tableau is limited by the value
theory which demands that the money circulation be congruent
with the value entity. All these concepts are now a commonplace
in the economist's bag of tools.

Most important, by helping to prick the conscience of the
Victorian world and to stir the fears of the Bismarckian regime,
Marx helped to further programs of social reform. He performed
the traditional service of the radical; although he overstated his
case, Marx documented the plight of the workingman and provided him with an ideology with which he might be aroused to
self-help.

Yet the positive initial effects of a theory does not necessarily
make for its scientific validity. In the long run, the criterion of
the use of knowledge for the improvement of human welfare depends on the scientific truth of the theory. The fact is that Marx
did predict the violent end of capitalism. Taken literally Marx
argued that crises would become more severe and the condition
of the working class would deteriorate until, either before or
after capitalism came to a complete collapse, the proletariat
would seize power. Moderates who attempted to "revise" Marx
from within the premises of his system came to grief as the
orthodox Marxists were able to cite chapter and verse from Marx
to support the extremist view. Lenin was able to argue that the
consequence of the materialist aspect of dialectical logic was
violent revolution and that consequently the Revisionists must
be cowards and opportunists.

Nevertheless, as the world socialist and labor movements developed into powerful social institutions the gadfly role of the
extremist radical lost its social usefulness. Inevitably the theoretical program of Marx came up for review. If, with Lenin and
Rosa Luxemburg, one felt that capitalism was inevitably going
to a destruction which would involve the working classes in a
catastrophic epoch of unemployment and imperialist war before
it finally ground to a halt, then capitalism's demise, like the mur-

der of Duncan, would best be accomplished quickly. Lenin would have it that the spot of blood would soon wash off. Class struggles should be intensified. The trade union and social reform movements should be seen as training grounds for revolution rather than ends in themselves. Therefore, the labor movement should be encouraged to press for their program in an increasingly militant demonstrative manner. Further, a consideration of democratic liberties as a social goal was meaningless, since the state has as its essence the maintenance of class rule. Democratic political forms, like unions, were not ends in themselves, but merely forms of class rule with which the proletariat might or might not encumber itself depending on its tactical convenience in the class struggle. For Lenin the centralism necessary to defeat a powerful ruling class which had not yet lost all its vitality required sacrifice of democratic rights of dissent to monolithic discipline.

But what if the evolution of capitalism brings a higher standard of living to the workers? Granted that this might in large part be due to the pressures of the organized labor movement itself. Nevertheless if the increases in productivity make a higher real wage possible and if fiscal and monetary policies maintain a reasonable degree of full employment, what can the orthodox Marxist advance as a reason for revolution? The argument for social change must now rest on the normative argument in what Karl Popper calls an "open society." In the absence of apodictic certainty that any policy or program is the correct one, one must argue for public policy that, in a *particular* instance, can be shown to increase the welfare of the majority. While precise criteria for maximizing social welfare are the subject of much current controversy among welfare economists, it is clear that the minority rights of dissent must be jealousy guarded. As John Strachey suggests in his *Contemporary Capitalism*,[5] as much room as possible must be left for retracing one's steps and revising programs in light of changing goals or new experience. It is not as Lenin would have it that socialism is the only goal and that hence violent revolution against an unyielding bourgeoisie is a necessity. Rather it is the democratic ideal and its political institutions which are paramount. If these can be maintained and enlarged then the real problem of increasing social welfare can be attacked.

Notes

Introduction

1. René Descartes, *Discourse on Method* in *The Philosophical Works of Descartes* trans. by E. S. Haldane and G. R. T. Ross (Cambridge, England, Cambridge University Press, 1911), I, 81–82.

2. Thorstein Veblen, "The Socialist Economics of Karl Marx and His Followers," *Quarterly Journal of Economics* (August, 1906).

3. Karl R. Popper, *The Logic of Scientific Discovery* (New York, Science Editions, 1961). This is the problem of the elimination of "psychologism" that Popper discusses. My essay owes a great deal to his work, especially the analysis of "essentialism" which he develops in *The Open Society and Its Enemies* and the *Poverty of Historicism*. I think his insistence on individual units of social analysis as opposed to "holism" makes his thesis throw out more of great value in social science than is necessary to maintain an empirical epistemology.

4. E.g., Robert Tucker, *Philosophy and Myth in Karl Marx* (Cambridge, England, Cambridge University Press, 1961).

5. George Lichteim, *Marxism, An Historical and Critical Study* (New York, Praeger, 1961).

6. For a contrary view see Daniel Bell, *The End of Ideology* (Glencoe, Ill., Free Press, 1960), Part III.

7. When we think of the psychological difficulties of being objective about Marxism we apply the first method of analysis to ourselves. Both Lichtheim and Hegel do not distinguish this from the second method which is concerned with the logical content of analysis. To them a theory must be of no current use to explain events or solve problems before it can be analyzed. It must be wrong.

It is amusing to note that Lichtheim's methodology which denies the significance of the two senses in which historical knowledge can be obtained is really a form of the logical paradox of some self-reflexive statement such as: Can it be true or false that "I am now lying"? Lichtheim uses the Hegelian doctrine to the effect that knowledge about ideas is available when they are no longer true. Yet Lichtheim assumes that the Hegelian doctrine is true *now*. Does this paradox not illustrate the inconsistency that one falls into if one denies the distinction between the psychological difficulty of objectively evaluating controversial material and the validity of its logical content? Actually, Lichtheim goes further in restraining the owl. Out of a distaste for, or lack of familiarity with, mathematics and economics he resorts to using Marxist theory when pressed to explain events (e.g., Lichtheim, p. 184).

If Lichtheim believes that Marxism in the first sense is irrelevant as an ideological force in world events, he simply is in flagrant contradiction to the facts. If he believes that it is wrong or obsolete as a method, his use of Marxian and earlier related methodologies makes him self-contradictory.

8. E.g., Joan Robinson, *An Essay on Marxian Economics* (London, Macmillan, 1942).

9. E.g., J. A. Schumpeter, *Capitalism, Socialism, and Democracy* (2d ed.; New York, Harper, 1947).

10. Karl Marx, *Capital,* (New York, Modern Library, 1906), I, 13.

11. Oscar R. Lange, "Marxian Economics and Modern Economic Theory," *Review of Economic Studies,* II, No. 3 (1935), 189–201.

12. M. Dobb, *Political Economy and Capitalism; Some Essays in Economic Tradition* (New York, International Publishers Co. Inc., 1945), p. 18. "This . . . is ultimately a practical and not a formal question. The truth of an economic principle must lie in whether, in making abstraction of certain aspects of the problem, it does so in order to focus upon features which are in fact crucial and fundamental features of that slice of the real world to which the theory is intended to apply."

13. K. Marx, *Economic and Philosophic Manuscripts of 1844* (Moscow, Foreign Language Publishing House, 1961).

14. E.g., Erich Fromm, *Marx's Concept of Man* (New York, Frederick Unger, 1961).

15. See Friedrich Engels, *Anti-Dühring* (Moscow, Foreign Language Publishing House, 1947): "the genesis and development of the mode of outlook expounded in this book were due in far greater measure to Marx, and only in an insignificant degree to myself, it was of course self-understood between us that this exposition of mine should not be issued without his knowledge. I read the whole manuscript to him before it was printed, and the tenth chapter of the section on economics . . . was written by Marx. . . . As a matter of fact, we had always been accustomed to help each other out in special subjects." Preface to 2d ed., p. 17.

Assuming that Engels is telling the truth and knowing what we do about Marx's assertiveness about his own views on theoretical questions, what sense can be made of a passage such as the following from Lichtheim? "The . . . medley of philosophy and science constitutes what has come to be known as 'dialectical materialism': a concept not present in the original Marxian version, and indeed essentially foreign to it, since for the early Marx the only nature relevant to the understanding of history is human nature. For the later Engels, on the contrary, historical evolution is an aspect of general (natural) evolution, and basically subject to the same 'laws.' The contrast could hardly be more glaring. That Marx put up with this travesty of his original standpoint is a factual circumstance which need not concern us, though it may be of interest to his biographers." Lichtheim, p. 245.

16. All this is so elementary and yet apparently it has to be repeated. In the prefaces to *Capital,* Marx is explicit: "One nation can and should learn from others. And even when a society has gone upon the right track for the discovery of the natural laws of its movement—and it is the ultimate aim of this work, to lay bare the economic law of motion of modern society—it can neither clear by bold leaps nor remove by legal enactments, the obstacles offered by the successive phases of its normal development. But it can shorten and lessen the birth pangs." Preface to the 1st ed. (1867), pp. 14–15. In the same preface Marx expresses his materialism in unmistakable terms: "My dialectic method is not only different from the Hegelian, but its direct opposite. To Hegel, the life-process of the human brain, i.e., the process of thinking, which, under the name of 'the Idea,' he even transforms into an independent subject, is the demiurgos of the real world, and the real world is only the external, phenomenal form of 'the Idea.' With me, on the contrary, the ideal is nothing else than the material world reflected by the human mind, and transformed into forms of thought." *Ibid.,* p. 25. Marx's proprietary use of the first person is in direct contrast to Lichtheim's interpretation.

17. See Chapter II which argues that subjective considerations are involved and therefore the theory is a failure.

Chapter I: Method

1. Thorstein Veblen, Review of Max Lorenz, *Die Marxistische Sozialdemokratie,* quoted in Joseph Dorfman, *Thorstein Veblen and His America* (New York, Viking, 1934), p. 146

2. Paul M. Sweezy, *The Theory of Capitalistic Development* (New

York, Oxford University Press, 1942) contains an excellent summary of the debate. This issue was first raised by Eduard Bernstein, in his *Evolutionary Socialism* (New York, Shocken, 1961).

3. E.g., Richard B. Braithwaite, *Scientific Explanation; A Study of the Function of Theory, Probability and Law in Science* (New York, Cambridge University Press, 1953); Karl R. Popper, *The Logic of Scientific Discovery* (London, Hutchinson, 1959) and *The Open Society and Its Enemies* (Princeton, N.J., Princeton University Press, 1950); Richard von Mises, *Positivism; A Study in Human Understanding* (New York, Braziller, 1956).

4. E.g., Friedrich Engels, *Ludwig Feuerbach and the Outcome of Classical German Philosophy* (New York, International Publishers Co. Inc., 1934).

5. In an attempt to reword this doctrine without recourse to jargon Georgiï Plekhanov produced a blunt thesis which Lenin said was the best statement of historical materialism, *The Materialistic Conception of History* (New York, International Publishers Co. Inc., 1940).

6. Hume anticipated this rational element in perception, but it remained for Kant to make it the center of his thesis.

7. This is the "model" of the econometrician; the basis from which he proceeds to statistically identify his variables.

8. See K. Popper, *The Poverty of Historicism* (London, Routledge, 1957), pp. 76 ff.

9. *Ibid.*, pp. 28 ff.

10. The distribution of income is not the same as the distribution of wealth. The latter is a matter of accumulation over history and is not directly price determined. In connection with long-run change, wealth must not be considered homogeneous; clearly landed wealth, or the investment of the *rentier* is of a different quality from the working capital of the entrepreneur.

11. The best explanation of the work of Hegel is to be found in W. T. Stace, *The Philosophy of Hegel; A Systematic Exposition* (New York, Dover, 1955).

12. Spinoza had argued that every singular determination of an object entailed the exclusion of all attributes other than those which belong to it. For every such class of predicates, U, there exists a class of not-U. Hegel extending Kant's insistence of the logical priority of categories and concepts of space-time claimed that all reality was ultimately a set of universals. Reality was thus ideal, the "thing-in-itself" a fiction, and particular events merely "moments" of the universals. Hegel claimed that by proving both the subsistent universal,

U, and its lack of self-subsistence, not-U, he would be defining a new classification with greater factual content. By continuing the process *ad infinitum,* in principle, one could arrive at the exclusion of universals which define the singular objects of experience.

13. Exactly what *is*ness is, is open to no little debate. Kant's refutation of the ontological proof of the existence of God explained that existence is not an attribute of an object. Rather it is merely a verbal device to introduce a predicate into a sentence. To Hegel, *is* does not really mean the existence of a particular object but that experience requires that ideas depend on a prior set of universals which in turn must depend on more general universals. Everything *is* in the same sense that Spinoza would have it that every object is *in* Substance.

14. Hegel had blurred the distinction between the content of thought (the fact that I am thinking about) and the thought itself (the fact that I am thinking). Both the content and the fact of thought may be designated by the same word but the meaning is different.

15. See Engels, *Anti-Dühring,* pp. 57–58.

16. By definition, the classification of attributes U and not-U, of the objects, means that we have defined no objects at all. The set of objects is empty. The statement not-U can serve as the boundary defining a set of objects, if U and not-U refer to different objects. If U is an absolute universal referring to *all* objects, then not-U cannot exist as its boundary. Hence if U (e.g., Being) is the only designation we give to *all* objects, then all we have said is that we cannot define any objects at all. There is, by hypothesis, not a not-U. All this would seem to say is that it is meaningless to talk about universals except as nominal generalizations from objective experience unless one were willing to dispense with experience altogether.

17. Ludwig Feuerbach, *The Essence of Christianity,* trans. by Marian Evans (3d ed; London, Kegan Paul, Trench, Trubner, & Co. Ltd., 1893). See also Frederick Copleston, *A History of Philosophy* (Westminster, Md., The Newman Press, 1963), Vol. VII, Fichte to Nietzsche.

18. Cf. Robert C. Tucker, *Philosophy and Myth in Karl Marx* (Cambridge, Eng., Cambridge University Press, 1961). Tucker does not fully appreciate this point and so misconstrues the deification of Man as an attempt of individuals to achieve divine moral perfection in the face of the knowledge of finite virtue. The resulting schizophrenia ends in the projection of individuals of mythical struggles between good and evil—between the individual Mr. Moneybags and

the proletarian in Marx. Kant, Hegel, Rousseau, Feuerbach, and Marx may have been wrong but they were quite sane investigators of the nature of the relation between individual thought as conditioned by universal categories or historical forces which are beyond their control. The carbuncles of Marx, unlike those of Job, resulted from malnutrition and the solid discomfort of the British Museum rather than the psychosomatic symptoms of the sin of Pride.

19. Marx, *Economic and Philosophic Manuscripts of 1844*, pp. 105–6. Marx is talking about capital, not the capital*ist* as Tucker imagines. As a matter of fact Marx says that with his preoccupation with *having*, the capitalist is also an unfulfilled victim of the institution of private property.

20. The Marshallian formulation of marginal utility escapes the two pitfalls of the earlier utility formulation. The use of marginal analysis avoids the paradox of value involved in attempting to equate the utility of diamonds and water in general without regard to the quantity of these commodities which the individual possesses. But more significantly for our point, the utility is individualized. It is not human satisfactions which are being compared but the schedules of satisfactions obtainable from different goods as they appear to each person at any instant of time. Thus *welfare economics* may tell us how satisfactions might be maximized, but does not show how the schedules of satisfactions arise.

21. "Bentham is a purely English phenomenon . . . in no time and in no country has the most homespun common-place ever strutted about in so self-satisfied way. The principle of utility was no discovery of Bentham. He simply reproduced in his dull way what Helvetius and other Frenchmen had said with esprit in the 18th century. To know what is useful for a dog, one must study dog-nature. This nature is not to be deduced from the principle of utility. Applying this to man, he that would criticize all human acts, movements, relations, etc., by the principle of utility, must first deal with human nature in general, and then with human nature as modified in each historical epoch. Bentham makes short work of it. With the dryest naivete he takes the modern shopkeeper, especially the English shopkeeper, as the normal man. What is useful to this queer normal man, and to his world, is absolutely useful. This yard-measure, then he applies to past, present and future. . . . Had I the courage of my friend, Heinrich Heine, I should call Mr. Jeremy a genius in the way of bourgeois stupidity." *Capital*, I, 668n.

22. K. Marx, *Theses on Feuerbach*, III and VI (Appendix in Engels,

Ludwig Feuerbach, pp. 73–75); cf. *The Communist Manifesto* published in January, 1848.

23. *Thesis* VI.

24. *Thesis* III.

25. "The chief defect of all hitherto existing materialism—that of Feuerbach included—is that the object . . . is conceived only in the form of *object* or *contemplation* but not as *human sensuous activity, practice,* not subjectively. . . . Feuerbach wants sensuous objects, really differentiated from the thought-objects, but he does not conceive human activity itself as activity *through objects.*" *Thesis* I.

26. It is revealing that of all the writings of Marx, the 1844 manuscripts alone are devoid of historical analysis.

27. Engels was not so cautious. See F. Engels, *Dialectics of Nature* (New York, International Publishers Co. Inc., 1940).

28. "Man himself, viewed as the impersonation of labor-power, is a natural object, a thing, although a living conscious thing, and labor is the manifestation of this power in him." *Capital,* I, 225 and cf. pp. 197–98.

29. These issues are summarized best by Marx in *Theses on Feuerbach.* See also V. I. Lenin, *Materialism and Empirio-Criticism* (Moscow, Foreign Languages Publishing House, 1947).

30. These are, of course, capital in the vocabulary of the "bourgeois economist," but not for Marx. Capital to Marx was the value which commands factors of production at this stage in historical evolution.

31. Note that Marx has excluded nonlabor factors as social costs at this early stage in his analysis by his monistic materialism. He is not speaking of subjective costs even of labor, but of expended material human effort.

32. This corresponds to the Hegelian category of "Lordship and Bondage" in G. W. F. Hegel, *Phenomenology of Mind* (London, Allen and Unwin, 1910), pp. 228–40.

33. Veblen's comments on the status of women and later of women captives suggests that barbarian society was not without its "honorific" class distinctions and exploitations. J. Dorfman, *Thorstein Veblen and His America* (New York, Viking, 1934), pp. 163–73.

34. M. M. Bober, *Karl Marx's Interpretation of History* (2d ed.; Cambridge, Mass., Harvard University Press, 1950).

35. The identification of the legal ideology of ownership with the real determinants of resource allocation has led to much mischief in comprehending the problems of the professionally managed corporation and those of socialist planning; cf. P. J. D. Wiles, *The Political*

Economy of Communism (Cambridge, Mass., Harvard University, 1960).

36. While Marx was not a Darwinian, as Veblen points out, it is interesting to speculate whether the Marxian system could be rescued by a theory of natural selection of tribal societies. Perhaps those that adopt the slave-latifundia agriculture survive over those that cling to the type of production which, in the agricultural stage, could be represented by the communal forms of the Russian *mir* or German *Mark*. Certainly within a slave society the production for exchange, military advantage, and the use of money and debt serve to undermine the tribal form. Engels' description of this process in the *Origin of the Family* is relevant here. But all this requires that slavery has proved more effective in the first instance. I would suggest that this may be true only under special geographic conditions such as the Mediterranean basin in which large-scale transportation for both military and commercial purposes by sea was fairly simple and where the terrain was adaptable to large-scale operations. For instance, large-scale irrigation projects might yield substantial returns in this area and would require not only large-scale farming but a complex centralized large-scale governmental apparatus. The extreme inequality in the distribution of income might be required to permit the savings of much of current income to supply the public capital. All this was subject to change when soil erosion and overgrazing reduced the profitability of these enterprises. But in other geographical environments the small-scale communal form not only preceded the slave-latifundia economy but lived alongside. In central and eastern Europe it became the basis for the feudal system in which the nobility took its tribute from the commune. This would tend to suggest that this small-scale agriculture was now not more efficient because of new technology but better adapted to a different geography.

37. F. Engels, *The Origin of the Family, Private Property and the State* (New York, International Publishers Co. Inc., 1940), pp. 136–37.

38. Max Weber, *General Economic History*, trans. by Frank H. Knight (Glencoe, Ill., The Free Press, 1927), chap. XII, pp. 275–78 and 334–37.

39. *Capital*, I, 89.

40. "Auguste Comte and his school might therefore have shown that feudal lords are an eternal necessity in the same way that they have done in the case of lords of capital." *Ibid.*, I, 365n. *Relative to the system* the imputed productivity of the nobility was a reality. What Marx is really saying is that there is a better system of providing

the social overhead. But this is the language of the reformer, not the revolutionary determinist. It depends on normative judgments and contingent facts, not demonstration.

Chapter II: Value

1. *Capital*, I, 93n.   2. *Ibid.*, I, 49.

3. George Stigler, "Ricardo and the 93% Labor Theory of Value," *American Economic Review*, XLVIII, No. 3 (1958), 357–67. For an argument that Ricardo had an absolute labor theory of value, see D. F. Gordon, "What Was the Labor Theory of Value," *American Economic Association Papers and Proceedings* (1959), pp. 452 ff.

4. E.g., Engels writes, "What therefore is the negation of the negation? An extremely general—and for this reason extremely comprehensive and important law of the development of Nature, history and thought; a law which, as we have seen, holds good in the animal and plant kingdoms, in geology, in mathematics and in philosophy. . . . It is obvious that in describing any evolutionary process as the negation of the negation I do not say anything concerning the particular process of development." F. Engels, *Herr Eugen Dühring's Revolution in Science (Anti-Dühring)* (Moscow, Foreign Language Publishing House, 1947), p. 210. Engels elaborates on this theme in this work (pp. 200 ff).

5. *Capital*, I, 43.

6. *Ibid.*, p. 45; cf. Eugen von Böhm-Bawerk *Karl Marx and the Close of His System* (New York, Augustus M. Kelley, 1949), pp. 68–69. Marx is here identified with "old Aristotle."

7. K. Popper, *The Open Society and Its Enemies* (Princeton, N.J., Princeton University Press, 1950). In a new book inspired by the work of Karl Popper, Mrs. Joan Robinson also concludes that *value* is a metaphysical concept devoid of empirical meaning. "It is," she says, "just a word." Joan Robinson, *Economic Philosophy* (Chicago, Aldine Publishing Company, 1963), p. 46.

8. *Capital*, I, 107–8.   9. *Ibid.*, I, 44.   10. *Ibid.*, I, 83.

11. This is the dispute between cardinal and ordinal utility initiated by J. R. Hicks, *Value and Capital* (2d ed.; London, Oxford University Press, 1946), chap. I.

12. *Capital*, I, 44.   13. *Ibid.*, I, 110.   14. *Ibid.*, I, 42.

15. *Ibid.*, III, 221.

16. While Marx may not have been aware of the overcoming of the technical difficulties of utility analysis by the marginalists, Engels was

at least conversant with it. In *Anti-Dühring* he remarks, "and . . . in economics it is assumed that every consumer is a real specialist in all the commodities which he has occasion to buy for his maintenance," p. 12. A criticism of marginal utility analysis is implied in this comment dated June, 1878. By October, 1894, in the introduction to Volume III of *Capital*, Engels refers directly to Jevons' and Menger's "theory of use value and marginal profit," p. 20.

17. *Capital*, I, 45. Marx did not trouble himself with the vexing problems of interpersonal and intertemporal comparisons of labor which bedeviled the utility theorists. It is a legitimate question whether the simple aggregation of money flows in national income accounting and its use as a welfare criterion is really conceptually superior to making normative economic judgments in terms of equally crude labor accounting. Of course Marx himself thought of labor value as much more than a useful index of welfare.

18. Böhm-Bawerk, p. 76. For a charming discussion of utility versus labor as the social universal, see the P. H. Wicksteed and G. B. Shaw interchange reprinted in Wicksteed, *The Common Sense of Political Economy* (New York, Augustus M. Kelley, 1950), II, 705–33.

19. M. Dobb, *Political Economy and Capitalism* (New York, International Publishers Co. Inc., 1945), p. 69.

20. R. Hilferding, *Böhm-Bawerk's Criticism of Marx* (New York, Augustus Kelley, 1949), pp. 138 ff.

21. *Capital*, I, 51–52, 52n.

22. If the isoquants were L-shaped reflecting the absolute complementarity of inputs, the points of tangency with a budget line would be at the kink regardless of the slope of the budget line, that is, regardless of the valuation of the factors of production.

23. *Capital*, I, 54n.

24. P. M. Sweezy, *The Theory of Capitalist Development* (New York, Oxford University Press, 1942), pp. 47–52.

25. *Capital*, I, 42.   26. *Ibid.*, I, 226.   27. *Ibid.*, III, 225.

28. *Ibid.*, III, 219.   29. *Ibid.*, III, 223–24.   30. *Ibid.*, I, 45.

31. *Ibid.*, I, 120–21.

32. Alfred Marshall, *Principles of Economics* (8th ed.; London, Macmillan, 1947), p. 814; cf; Mark Blaug, *Ricardian Economics* (New Haven, Conn., Yale University Press, 1958), pp. 14–15.

33. *Capital*, III, 211.

34. K. Marx, *Theories of Surplus Value*, selections (New York, International Publishers Co. Inc., 1952), p. 246.

35. This issue is extensively discussed in the literature starting with

Marshall's Appendix H, where the possible incompatibility of perfect competition and decreasing cost with stable prices and outputs is discussed. Henderson and Quandt provide the demonstration that the output of the firm is unstable if it has an homogeneous production function of degree one. J. M. Henderson and R. E. Quandt, *Microeconomic Theory* (New York, McGraw-Hill, 1958), pp. 66–67.

36. Marshall, pp. 817–19.   37. *Ibid.*, p. 810.

38. $W = \dfrac{1}{L} \displaystyle\int_0^L (s_2)\, dq$

39. *Capital*, III, 210.

40. K. Marx, *Das Kapital* (Hamburg, Otto Meissner, 1894), Vol. III, Pt. 1, pp. 157–58.

41. K. Marx, *Theories of Surplus Value*, pp. 246–48.

42. *Capital*, III, 220–21.

43. *Ibid.*, III, 213–14.

44. J. R. Hicks, *Value and Capital* (2d ed.; London, Oxford University Press, 1946), pp. 26 ff. Cf. M. A. Dobb, "A Sceptical View of the Theory of Wages," *Economic Journal* (December, 1929), reprinted in *On Economic Theory and Socialism* (New York, International Publishers, 1955); D. H. Robertson, "Wage Grumbles," in *Economic Fragments*, reprinted in W. Fellner and B. F. Haley, eds., *Readings in the Theory of Income Distribution* (Philadelphia, Blakiston, 1940), pp. 42–57.

45. *Capital*, I, 586 ff.

46. Assume each firm wishes to maximize its production, *P*, within the constraint provided by the effort that the labor-enterpreneur wishes to expend, *B*. Introducing the Lagrange multiplier λ we form the equation

$$Z = K(x_0 + a_1x_1 + \ldots + a_ix_i + a_jx_j + \ldots + a_nx_n + C)$$
$$+ \lambda(B - L(x_0, x_1, \ldots, x_i, x_j, \ldots, x_n, C))$$

and maximize *P* by setting partial derivatives equal to zero. We need to consider only the variables x_i and x_j and

$$Ka_i - \lambda \frac{\partial L}{\partial x_i} = 0,$$

$$Ka_j - \lambda \frac{\partial L}{\partial x_j} = 0,$$

$$\lambda = \frac{Ka_i}{\partial L/\partial x_i} = \frac{Ka_j}{\partial L/\partial x_j},$$

and

$$\frac{a_i}{a_j} = \frac{\partial x_j}{\partial x_i}.$$

J. M. Henderson and R. E. Quandt, p. 270; William F. Osgood, *Advanced Calculus* (New York, Macmillan, 1925).

47. The question of homogeneity and its degree, that is, whether they are equally spaced, is not required for this discussion, but arises implicitly in the discussion of demand later in this chapter.

48. Since

$$dx_j = \frac{a_i}{a_j} dx_i,$$

we may integrate, and

$$x_j = \frac{a_i}{a_j} x_i + C.$$

When $x_j = 0$ then x_i is also zero since the equivalent of zero labor, x_j, must also be zero labor. Hence $C = 0$, and

$$x_j = \frac{a_i}{a_j} x_i.$$

If $i = 0$ for simple labor, $a_0 = 1$, then

$$a_j x_j = x_0,$$

where $a_j > 1$. The labor value added by concrete labor time, x_j, is shown to be a multiple of simple labor x_0 as a result of their respective marginal productivities.

49. In order to show the conditions for maximizing production subject to the budget constraint, $B = L (x_0, \ldots ,x_i, \ldots ,x_n, C)$, we utilize the Lagrange multiplier λ to form the function

$$V = P[x_0, \ldots, x_i, x_j, \ldots, x_n, C] + \lambda[B - L(x_0, \ldots, x_i, x_j, \ldots, x_n, C)].$$

Here C represents the constant capital. Maximizing by setting partial derivatives equal to zero, we obtain

$$\frac{\partial V}{\partial x_i} = \frac{\partial P}{\partial x_i} - \lambda \frac{\partial L}{\partial x_i} = 0,$$

$$\frac{\partial V}{\partial x_j} = \frac{\partial P}{\partial x_j} - \lambda \frac{\partial L}{\partial x_j} = 0.$$

Solving these equations for λ, we obtain

$$\frac{\partial P/\partial x_i}{\partial L/\partial x_i} = \frac{\partial P/\partial x_j}{\partial L/\partial x_j} = \lambda$$

or

$$\frac{P_i}{L_i} = \frac{P_j}{L_j}.$$

Equilibrium requires that the individual laborer must be able to compare his own marginal physical product with an estimate of the subjective cost of his own efforts.

If, alternatively, the conditions were rewritten as

$$\frac{P_i}{P_j} = \frac{L_i}{L_j},$$

then, while the left member would be technological, the right-hand side of the equation requires that the laborer still evaluate his own effort in comparison to alternative occupations or combinations of different amounts of time spent in different productive operations. In terms of the rate of technical substitution the marginal disutilities of work are

$$\frac{dx_i}{dx_j} = \frac{L_j}{L_i}.$$

Hence x_i and x_j are related by some function satisfying the integral equation

$$\int L_j \, dx_j = \int L_i \, dx_i.$$

50. The case of increasing costs presents problems of nonlabor increments in value which we will discuss in the section of this chapter devoted to the problem of demand.

51. What follows is an adaptation of the problem of aggregation as discussed R. G. D. Allen, *Mathematical Economics* (New York, St. Martin's Press, 1957), pp. 697 ff. The mathematical implications are discussed in greater detail there and further references are given.

52. This can be illustrated by assuming hypothetical values. Let us take two industries, I and II, valuing labors x_i and x_j according to their respective reduction ratios which we take to be

$$\text{I: } 2x_i = 5x_j,$$
$$\text{II: } x_i = x_j.$$

The weighted sum of x_i and x_j is the aggregation of the two equations. It gives $3x_i = 6x_j$ and the average reduction ratio $x_i/x_j = 2$. If we aggregate by the second method and solve for x_i/x_j then

$$3x_i = \tfrac{5}{2}(2x_j)$$

and $x_i/x_j = 5/3$. Furthermore, if we increase x_j by Δx_j then

$$\text{I: } 2x_i + 5\Delta x_j = 5(x_j + \Delta x_j),$$
$$\text{II: } x_i + \Delta x_j = x_j + \Delta x_j.$$

By aggregating by the first method the average ratio remains 2 since $3x_i + 6\Delta x_j = 6x_j + 6\Delta x_j$ and $x_i/x_j = 2$. But if we average by the second method, we obtain

$$3x_i + 6\Delta x_j = (\tfrac{5}{2})(2x_j + 2\Delta x_j),$$
$$3x_i = 5x_j - \Delta x_j,$$

$$\frac{x_i}{x_j} = \frac{5}{3} - \frac{\Delta x_j}{3x_j}.$$

The error introduced as a result of improper aggregation increases in direct proportion to the percentage increase in the use of x_j.

53. I am greatly indebted to Professor Eugene Rotwein for conversations in which he probed into an earlier inadequate formulation of this question.

54. We form the function Z equal to the linear production function plus a Lagrange multiplier times the budgetary constraint

$$B = k + v_o + \ldots + v_i + v_j + \ldots + v_n,$$
$$Z = P(x_0 + a_1 x_1 + \ldots + a_i x_i + a_j x_j) + \lambda(B - (k + v_0 + \ldots + v_i + v_j)).$$

When one remembers: $v_i = a_i x_i / \sigma_i$, since $\sigma_i = a_i x_i / v_i$ and

$$\frac{\partial P}{\partial x_i} + \lambda \frac{a_i}{\sigma_i} = 0,$$

then

$$\frac{\partial P}{\partial x_j} + \lambda \frac{a_j}{\sigma_j} = 0.$$

But since $\partial P/\partial x_i = a_i$ and $\partial P/\partial x_j = a_j$, where

$$a_i + \frac{\lambda a_i}{\sigma_i} = 0 = a_j + \frac{\lambda a_j}{\sigma_j},$$

Marx requires that $-\lambda = \sigma_i = \sigma_j = \ldots$. The equilibrium condition requires that the rate of surplus value be equalized for all types of concrete labor.

55. The marginal productivity of a is $\partial W/\partial_a = x'$.

56. Marx saw that it is impossible to determine the value of different labors by examining their wages and at the same time derive their rates of surplus value from the difference between wage and value of product. See *Capital* I, 51–52.

57. Sweezy, p. 65.

58. *Capital,* III, 206.

Chapter III: The Wage Bargain

1. At least this is the way Marx read Smith and Ricardo. There is considerable debate as to whether Smith or Ricardo meant to ascribe all value to labor. Smith can be read as attributing value to labor only under the primitive conditions of barter of deer for beaver. George Stigler suggests that Ricardo only meant to use labor as an index of value which was closer to an invariant standard than any other. These issues are irrelevant, however, to Marx's conclusions. Marx saw these reservations of the classical economists as inconsistencies rather than misgivings about the labor theory of value. Cf. David Ricardo, *The Works and Correspondence of David Ricardo*, ed. P. Sraffa (Cambridge, England, Cambridge University Press, 1951), I, xxxvii.

2. *Capital*, I, 588–89n. 3. *Ibid.*, I, 115.

4. *Ibid.*, Vol. III, Part V. 5. *Ibid.*, II, 33.

6. Mrs. Joan Robinson points out that Marx must have the labor performed involved in the wage bargain in order to equalize the rate of surplus value between firms. Assuming all other things equal (that is, turnover rates and particularly the organic composition of capital), the rate of profit of a firm is determined by the ratio of labor time expended for the capitalist (surplus value) and that for the reproduction of the subsistence of the laborers (variable capital). Since this cannot be unequal between firms the wage bargain must be an equilibrium between some function of the labor performed and the wage rate. But labor power has a value determined by the subsistence cost of reproducing the laborer and not by the total product he produces. The theory advanced by Marx does not correspond to either the facts of bargaining or the need for a uniform rate of profit. Further, since the employment of labor power to produce surplus value is its use value as opposed to the exchange (labor) value of a commodity, it is clear that the wage bargain is determined by use value rather than exchange value. Clearly the value concept comes to grief as an explanation of the value of labor and ought to be replaced by a theory of price. (See my discussion of the reduction of concrete to simple labor in a wage economy in Chapter II.)

7. *Ibid.*, I, 587. 8. *Ibid.*, I, 186. 9. *Ibid.*, I, 186.

10. *Ibid.*, I, 185–86. 11. *Ibid.*, I, 70.

12. E. g., J. A. Schumpeter, "The Analysis of Economic Change" *Review of Economic Studies*, XVII, No. 4 (May 1935). Reprinted in *Readings in Business Cycle Theory* (Homewood, Ill., R. D. Irwin, 1951), p. 1.

13. *Capital,* I, 422–23; cf. W. J. Baumol, *Economic Dynamics* (New York, Macmillan, 1959), chap. II.

14. Hegel interpreted this as the *concept* of man trying to *know* the external world. Labor was the source of human knowledge.

15. *Capital,* I, 558.   16. *Ibid.,* I, 588.

17. P. M. Sweezy, *The Theory of Capitalist Development* (New York, Oxford University Press, 1942), pp. 84–85.

18. *Capital,* I, 667 f.   19. *Ibid.,* I, 190.

20. *Ibid.,* I, 669.   21. *Ibid.,* I, 707.

22. Marx recognizes important qualifications and counteracting causes such as lower prices for goods consumed by the working class which may mean greater flows of commodities to them at the same or higher levels of satisfaction. He treats these in his theory of relative surplus value, which is discussed below in this chapter.

23. *Ibid.,* I, 82 *passim.* It should be mentioned that Marx saw that not all of this value necessarily had to be used in productive consumption but, anticipating Keynes, argued that it might be hoarded in money form. Marx did not follow this up to develop an equilibrium theory of liquidity preference, he confined the influence of the liquid cash balance to the period of crisis. We may thus regard the aggregate demand as the amount of value available.

24. Cf. Oscar R. Lange, *Price Flexibility and Employment* (Bloomington, Ind., Principia Press, 1944); J. R. Hicks, *Value and Capital* (2d ed.; Oxford, Clarendon Press, 1946), pp. 316, 333–35.

25. The propensity to consume may turn out to be the short-run monetary equivalent for the wage to national income ratio. The similarity between Marx's constant rate of surplus value, the constant long-run share of wages in income found by Douglas, and the long-run constancy of the *average* propensity to consume found by Goldsmith, Kuznets, and Friedman is striking.

26. Cf. Joan Robinson, "The Basic Theory of Normal Prices, *Quarterly Journal of Economics,* LXXVI, No. 1 (1962), 12–13.

27. Of course sticky money wages would not necessarily be compatible with full employment if demand falls.

28. J. A. Schumpeter, *Capitalism, Socialism and Democracy* (New York, Harper, 1942).

29. Its closest relative is Keynes liquidity preference explanation of interest. The supply of liquid money is limited by the state, and its value does not rise because of sticky money wage and prive levels. The labor theory of value serves the same function for Marx as does wage money illusion for Keynes.

30. *Capital*, Vol. I, Part V.

31. Cf. Paul Wonnacott, "Disguised and Overt Unemployment in Underdeveloped Countries," *Quarterly Journal of Economics*, LXXVI, No. 2 (1962), 279 ff.

32. J. Robinson, *An Essay on Marxian Economics* (London, Macmillan, 1942), p. 45.

33. *Ibid.*, p. 42. The falling rate of profit will be discussed in the next chapter.

34. *Capital*, I, 573.

35. The possibility of a single buyer of labor restricting employment in order to buy labor at lower prices is the notion of exploitation proposed by Mrs. Robinson in the *Economics of Imperfect Competition*. This is not excluded in the present analysis; nor is the possibility of discriminating monopsony reducing P to V even under conditions of rising supply price of labor. Exploitation to Marx, however, was a creature of perfect competition which is exacerbated by monopoly.

36. *Capital*, Vol. I, chap. XXV, sec. 3, pp. 689 ff.

37. *Ibid.*, III, 260.   38. *Ibid.*, III, 261–62.

39. *Ibid.*, Vol. II, Part II, pp. 173 ff.

40. *Ibid.*, I, 682, 689.

41. *Ibid.*, I, 689. One might remark in passing that monopoly as it represents vertical integration tends to economize on the limited supply of capital as conceived of by Marx. For gross product $C + V + S$ contains an element of double counting in that the C represents purchases between capitalists. The more atomized the production process is the greater the number of times C must be counted as the capital available for accumulation tied up in dead labor. Of course this argument is based on a technical weakness in Marx's concept of national product rather than on any question of fact.

42. *Ibid.*, I, 560.   43. *Ibid.*, I, 562.   44. *Ibid.*, I, 565.

45. *Ibid.*, I, 566.   46. Sweezy, p. 49.   47. *Capital*, I, 680.

48. *Ibid.*, I, 699.   49. *Ibid.*, III, 293.   50. *Ibid.*, III, 292.

51. See P. A. Samuelson, "Economists and the History of Ideas," *American Economic Review*, LII, No. 1 (1962), 13–14.

52. Baumol, pp. 130 ff.

53. Kenneth E. Boulding, *Economic Analysis* (3d ed.; New York, Harper, 1955), chap. 37; and B. F. Haley, ed., *A Survey of Contemporary Economics* (Homewood, Ill., R. D. Irwin, Inc., 1952), II, 14 ff.

54. The actual originator was Edgeworth from whom Boulding borrowed the diagram to illustrate the wage bargain.

Chapter IV: Crises

1. If the rate of growth of constant capital exceeds the growth of total capital, then

$$\frac{\Delta c}{c} > \frac{\Delta(c + v)}{c + v}$$

and

$$\frac{\Delta c}{c} - \frac{\Delta(c + v)}{c + v} = k$$

where $k > 0$. Performing the subtraction, we obtain

$$\frac{v\Delta c - c\Delta v}{c(c + v)} = k$$

and

$$v\Delta c - c\Delta v = kc(c + v).$$

Since $c(c + v) > 0$ and $k > 0$; $v\Delta c > c\Delta v$ and $\Delta c/\Delta v > c/v$ and

$$\frac{\Delta(c + v)}{\Delta v} > \frac{c + v}{v} \therefore \frac{\Delta v}{v} > \frac{\Delta(c + v)}{c + v}.$$

(If we have absolute overproduction of capital, that is, $\Delta(c + v) = 0$, then since $v > 0, \Delta v < 0$.)

2. See the discussion of Henryk Grossman in P. M. Sweezy, *The Theory of Capitalist Development* (New York, Oxford University Press, 1942), pp. 209–13.

3. *Capital*, III, 261.

4. Joseph M. Gillman, *The Falling Rate of Profit, Marx's Law and Its Significance to Twentieth-Century Capitalism* (London, Dennis Dobson, 1957), p. 149.

5. *Capital*, III, 294–95. The *possibility* of constant or declining wages along with decline in profit rate under conditions similar to those described by Marx is discussed in terms of physical productivity in a Cobb-Douglas production function by William Fellner, "Marxian Hypotheses and Observable Trends under Capitalism: a Modern Interpretation," *Economic Journal*, LXVII, No. 265 (1957), 16–20. Fellner argues that given increases in (constant) capital *only*, its marginal productivity will fall. This version of diminishing returns says that static or even slowly changing technology or the monopolistic shifting of income from wages to profit could not restore the old profit rate. The real issue, however, Fellner says is not the static problem of diminishing returns and factor combination, but depends on the counteracting effects of increases in productivity. For a similar analysis

which minimizes the counteracting causes, see H. D. Dickinson, "The Falling Rate of Profit in Marxian Economics," *Review of Economic Studies*, XXIV, No. 64 (1957), 120–30.

6. J. R. Hicks, *A Contribution to the Theory of the Trade Cycle* (London, Oxford University Press, 1950).

7. I shall discuss underconsumption as a possible independent cause of crises below.

8. *Capital*, III, 294.

9. Sweezy suggests this under the influence of the stagnation variant of the Keynesian analysis. Sweezy, Pt. III.

10. *Capital*, III, 298–99.

11. *Ibid.*, III, 298. 12. *Ibid.*, III, 299.

13. See K. Marx, *Theories of Surplus Value* (New York, International Publishers Co. Inc., 1952), p. 372.

14. K. Marx and F. Engels, *The Communist Manifesto* (New York, International Publishers Co. Inc., 1948), pp. 14–15.

15. See Sweezy, Pt. III. Sweezy attributes the doctrine of increasing severity of crises to Kautsky. I think, however, it is central to Marx's notion of the breakdown of capitalism.

16. *Capital*, Vol. III, Part III, chaps. 13–15.

17. *Ibid.*, III, 68, 102n.

18. By differentiating, we obtain $dp' = q'ds' + s'dq'$. For Marx $ds' = 0$ since the rate of surplus value is constant and hence the rate of change in the profit rate $dp' = s'dq'$. Hence if the organic composition of capital rises, $dq' < 0$ and hence $dq' < 0$ also. The rate of profit and q' can be shown to have the same critical points by setting $dp' = 0$. But then $dq' = 0$ also. These, moreover, are both maxima as can be seen by differentiating again, whence

$$d^2p' = s'\ d^2q' + dq'\ ds'.$$

Since $ds' = 0$ and $s' > 0$, d^2p' and d^2q' have the same sign.

19. *Capital*, III, 182–83.

20. *Ibid.*, III, 280; See pp. 196–97, 269, 272.

21. *Ibid.*, III, 248. 22. *Ibid.*, III, e.g., p. 249.

23. *Ibid.*, III, 277. 24. Gillman, p. 6.

25. M. Dobb, *Political Economy and Capitalism* (New York, International Publishers Co. Inc., 1949), p. 122.

26. Rosa Luxemburg, *The Accumulation of Capital*, trans. by A. Schwarzschild (New Haven, Conn., Yale University Press, 1951).

27. V. I. Lenin, *Selected Works* (New York, International Publishers Co. Inc., 1943), X, 312–13.

28. V. I. Lenin, *Imperialism, The Highest Stage of Capitalism, A Popular Outline, Selected Works* (New York, International Publishers Co. Inc., 1943), V, 56–60.

29. Sweezy, p. 205.   30. Luxemburg, p. 132.

31. Sweezy, pp. 183 ff.

32. Evsey D. Domar, "The Problem of Capital Accumulation" *American Economic Review*, XXXVIII, No. 5 (1948), 790. By capital Domar means constant capital, and he prefers to speak of total demand for output, income, rather than consumption as Sweezy does.

33. *Ibid.* The demonstration referred to is Domar's "Capital Expansion, Rate of Growth and Employment," *Econometrica*, XIV (1946), 137–47.

34. Domar's articles have been reprinted in Evsey D. Domar, *Essays in the Theory of Economic Growth* (New York, Oxford University Press, 1957).

35. See Paul A. Samuelson, "Marxian Economic Models," *American Economic Review*, XLVII, No. 6 (1957), 897–98. While Samuelson's demonstration of the necessity of a rise in real wages with a fall in profits is not derived from Marx's own premise, he does provide the translation of Marxian reproduction schemes into a dynamic Harrod-Domar model.

36. Robert Solow, "The Contribution to the Theory of Economic Growth," *Quarterly Journal of Economics*, LXX, No. 1 (1956), 64–94

37. Marx, *Theories of Surplus Value*, p. 377, italics added.

38. Oscar R. Lange, "Say's Law, A Restatement and Criticism" in *Studies in Mathematical Economics and Econometrics* (Chicago, University of Chicago Press, 1942), pp. 49–68.

39. Marx, *Theories of Surplus Value*, p. 392.

40. *Capital*, III, 286.   41. *Ibid.*, II, 475–76.

42. Marx, *Theories of Surplus Value*, pp. 386–87.

43. These terms are Hegel's; they express the need for an evolutionary necessity (notion) to subsume science and causation (understanding) in it.

44. Marx, *Theories of Surplus Value*, p. 387.

45. *Ibid.*, pp. 387–88.

Chapter V: Revisionism and Proletarian Revolution

1. Eduard Bernstein, *Evolutionary Socialism* (New York, Shocken Books, 1961), pp. 209–10.

2. V. I. Lenin, *Marxism and Revisionism,* Selected Works (New York, International Publishers Co. Inc., 1943), XI, 709, 711.

3. See A. K. Cairncross, "Internal Migration in Victorian England," in *Home and Foreign Investment 1870–1913, Studies in Capital Accumulation* (London, Cambridge University Press, 1953), chap. IV, pp. 73–77.

4. Bernstein's book was a formalization of ideas presented to the Stuttgart Congress of the German Social-Democrat Party in 1898.

5. Bernstein, p. 144.   6. *Ibid.*

7. See Oscar R. Lange and Fred M. Taylor, *On the Economic Theory of Socialism,* ed. Benjamin E. Lippincott (New York, McGraw-Hill, 1938); L. Von Mises, "Economic Calculation in a Socialist Commonwealth" in F. A. Hayek, ed., *Collectivist Economic Planning* (London, Routledge, 1935).

8. Von Mises, p. 80. Kautsky carried this argument even further to world monopoly organization. The inconsistency here ultimately turns on the likelihood of the optimum allocation of resources taking place under perfectly competitive "anarchy of production."

9. For example, Paul A. Samuelson's address to American Bankers Association: *Proceedings of a Symposium on Economic Growth,* February 25, 1963. (New York, The American Banker's Association, 1963), pp. 79 ff.

10. F. Engels, *Origin of the Family, Private Property and the State* (New York, International Publishers Co. Inc., 1942).

11. V. I. Lenin, *State and Revolution* (New York, International Publishers Co. Inc., 1942), III, 15.

12. *Ibid.,* III, 18.

13. P. M. Sweezy, *The Theory of Capitalist Development* (New York, Oxford University Press, 1942), pp. 239 ff.

14. V. I. Lenin, *Left-Wing Communism, An Infantile Disorder,* (New York, International Publishers Co. Inc., 1943), Vol. X of Selected Works.

15. V. I. Lenin, *What is to Be Done?* (New York, International Publishers Co. Inc., 1943), Vol. II of Selected Works.

16. V. I. Lenin, *Imperialism, the Highest Stage of Capitalism* (New York, International Publishers Co. Inc., 1943), Vol. V of Selected Works.

17. *Ibid.,* p. 80.

18. See W. W. Rostow, *The Process of Economic Growth* (New York, W. W. Norton Co., 1962), chap. XIII, p. 328–31.

19. See Joe S. Bain, "Economies of Scale, Concentration and Entry," *American Economic Review,* XLIV, No. 1 (1954), 15–39. In this

well-known study Professor Bain suggests that there are a significant number of firms in which internal economies have led to a large market share being attributed to a single plant of optimal size. He is less certain as to the economies of multiplant firms.

20. *Capital*, I, 686–87. Marx also notes the opposite tendency at work in the "fractionalization" of capital by the development of new firms. But he anticipates this tendency to be weaker than the concentration and centralization. Bernstein's challenge to the extrapolation of Marx's nineteenth-century observation is attacked by Lenin who argues that control remains in the hands of the larger units due to their absolute size rather than the percentage of capital actually in their hands.

21. Obviously the enduring importance of this institution as a device for the concentration of economic power was greatly overestimated by these writers.

22. Sweezy, pp. 272–74.

23. David Ricardo, *Principles of Political Economy and Taxation* (London, J. M. Dent and Sons, Everyman Library, 1911), p. 77; Marx, *Capital*, III, 278–79; and M. H. Dobb, *Political Economy and Capitalism* (New York, International Publishers Co. Inc., 1945), p. 227.

24. See Dobb, pp. 225–33.

25. Exchange value wages also might be heightened if we were to accept Marx's version of foreign trade over Ricardo's. See note 23.

26. It is this circumstance which prevents a simple statistical test of the increasing misery doctrine in terms of a single nation's real wage.

27. Lenin, *Imperialism*, p. 90.   28. Rostow, p. 42.

29. *Ibid.*, p. 331. The placing of income taxes "above all" is a surprisingly naïve statement coming from such a perceptive observer.

30. An analysis of the 1962 Supreme Court implementation of the significantly broadened definition of the types of mergers that are prohibited by the Celler-Kefauver Act (1950) amendments to the Clayton Act is to be found in David D. Martin, "The Brown Shoe Case and the New Antimerger Policy," *American Economic Review*, LIII, No. 3 (1963), 240–358.

31. Lenin, *Imperialism*, pp. 62–63.   32. Bernstein, pp. 179–80.

33. Joseph Stalin, *Foundations of Leninism* (New York, International Publishers Co. Inc., 1939), chap. I, pp. 13–19.

34. Cairncross, p. 121. Analyzing the British census of 1908 Cairncross estimates that of net saving of £285 thousand, £150 thousand went to net home investment and £135 thousand overseas. He argues that much of domestic capital formation was a widening of the stock

of capital to keep up with the demand for consumer goods arising from the population growth and the expansion of real income. Both population and income were stimulated, Cairncross says, by the low price of imports into the British Isles. *Ibid.,* p. 7. Housing, for instance, absorbed half of the total fixed capital formation. *Ibid.,* p. 120. He goes on to argue, however, that the contribution of investment abroad to effective demand in Britain is impossible to measure. Investment might have been a "sink" for excess savings which could not have been invested profitably in the domestic economy. *Ibid.,* pp. 232 ff. J. M. Keynes at least once supported the view suggested in the text, *viz.* R. F. Harrod, *The Life of John Maynard Keynes* (New York, Harcourt, 1951), pp. 346–53.

35. I am grateful to Professor Richard E. Towey of Oregon State University for his suggestion that this qualification is necessary. Clearly this question needs further empirical exploration.

36. Samuel Pizer and Frederick Cutler, *U.S. Business Investments in Foreign Countries* (Washington, D.C., U.S. Department of Commerce, Office of Business Economics, 1960). See also the summary articles by the same authors in the *Survey of Current Business* (Washington, D.C., U.S. Department of Commerce, September–October, 1960). As significant as the fact that nonexploitative investments are welcomed, is the evidence that these private investments are forthcoming.

37. Pizer and Cutler, *U.S. Business Investments in Foreign Countries,* p. 1.

38. Data are available on employment for 1957. Percentages of total are calculated below for both book value and employment by

Percent of Total U.S. Investment Overseas Measured
by Book Value of Assets and Employment
(1957)

	Book Value	Employment
Manufacturing	32	53
Petroleum	36	11
Mining and Smelting	10	6
Public Utilities	8	4
Other Industries	14	26

Source: Adapted from Pizer and Cutler, *U.S. Business Investment in Foreign Countries,* p. 123.

industry. Department of Commerce reports that in 1957 the next fixed assets of world U.S. investments in petroleum were valued at $8,200 million as compared to $4,962 million current assets. The manufacturing position was almost the reverse, with $5,817 million fixed and $8,207 million current (*ibid.*, pp. 26–28, 80, 195).

39. *Ibid.*, p. 78.

40. All of the preceding should not be construed to minimize the formidable problems of industrialization. A pathetic commentary is to be found in the *net* direct investment figures. It appears that there are large negative direct investments of the United States in such nations as Dominican Republic, Honduras, and in some years South Africa, Mexico, and Panama. Local personages invest in U.S. business faster than they import capital. The amounts involved are quite large. *Ibid.*, pp. 136–37.

41. Committee for Economic Development, *Cooperation for Progress in Latin America* (New York, C.E.D., 1961), pp. 10–11.

42. *Ibid.*, p. 40.

43. See Stalin, pp. 15–16; Lenin, *Imperialism*, pp. 92–93.

Chapter VI: Conclusions

1. J. S. Mill, *Autobiography of John Stuart Mill* (New York, Columbia University Press, paperback edition, 1960), pp. 120–21, 149.

2. *Ibid.*, pp. 114–18; cf. Jacques Barzun, *Darwin, Marx, Wagner* (New York, Doubleday, 1958), for the view of the cultural historian. While Barzun's book supports the thesis presented in this book, unfortunately its tone is extremely personal and on occasion vindictive.

3. Alfred Marshall, *Principles of Economics* (8th ed.; London, Macmillan, 1927), Preface to 1st ed., p. ix.

4. Cf. M. Blaug, *Ricardian Economics* (New Haven, Conn., Yale University Press, 1958), pp. 34–37; H. M. Robertson and W. L. Taylor, "Adam Smith's Approach to the Theory of Value," *Economic Journal*, LXVII, No. 266 (1957), 181–98.

5. John Strachey, *Contemporary Capitalism* (New York, Random House, 1956).

Index